WEDNESDAY NIGHT AT EIGHT

Wednesday Night at Eight

RICHARD & SUE HAYDON-KNOWELL

KINGSWAY PUBLICATIONS
EASTBOURNE

ISBN 0 86065 347 1

Biblical quotations are from
the New International Version, © New York International
Bible Society 1978.

To our house-group leaders
and their wives
who have taught us
so much

Printed in Great Britain for
KINGSWAY PUBLICATIONS LTD
Lottbridge Drove, Eastbourne, E. Sussex BN23 6NT by
Cox & Wyman Ltd, Reading
Typeset by Nuprint Services Ltd, Harpenden, Herts.

Contents

Acknowledgements

Our warm thanks are due to a large number of people: to Coastlands Trust for allowing us to use material already published; to the lovely ladies in our church who baked cakes and puddings for us every weekend, freeing Sue to write during the week; to Maggie Foss, Ron and Audrey Hopgood, and Norman and Margaret Moss, who supplied their homes as 'quiet places' in which to write; and to Janis, Richard's secretary, who patiently typed and re-typed the manuscript. Thank you, too, to our house-group leaders, many of whom are mentioned in this book; they have been the 'guinea pigs' for much of the teaching given here.

Our greatest thanks and gratitude go to our Lord Jesus Christ, the head of his church, who is still leading his people and empowering them by his Spirit to put into practice the principles taught in his word. That is what this book is all about.

Introduction

We have written this book out of sixteen years' pastoral experience in an evangelical, independent church in South London. We came to the church in December 1968 with our three and three-quarter children (the fourth was born soon after we arrived!) and settled into fairly uneventful pastoral life. In 1972 God began to move in the church in a new way; church members who had for years been doctrinally sound but lacking in spiritual power began to receive the baptism in the Holy Spirit. They became hungry for God and his word, for deep fellowship with him and with one another, for holiness of life and for freedom in praise and worship.

During the next few years, as the church came alive in the Spirit and began to grow, the need for more leadership became apparent. At that time Richard was the only full-time pastor; although he was helped by several elders who were in secular jobs and thus had only limited time to devote to church leadership.

In 1977 we decided to form house groups so that the church members could receive greater individual teaching and care. We divided into five house groups each of about eighteen members. Shortly afterwards another elder was appointed, and in 1980 he came into full-time pastoral leadership with Richard. By 1984 we had grown to twelve house groups and membership of the church was around two hundred.

At the time of writing we are in the process of joining with another local fellowship to make one new church, which will have three full-time pastoral elders and three elders who also have secular jobs. We will have eighteen house groups meeting in the area. God is continuing to increase our number as people come to faith in Christ, and it is exciting to be part of a growing, vibrant church; exciting, too, to see men coming into house-group leadership and becoming more mature and strong Christians as they learn to function in this role.

In this book we have set out many of the principles we have taught in the house-group leaders' training sessions over these years. Our aim is to show that well-taught men in house-group leadership can benefit a church immeasurably and that a far higher standard of individual care can be achieved than is possible with one or even two full-time pastors.

This book is about house-group life and leadership. Part One is for house-group leaders, but will also be helpful to house-group members who want to gain as much as possible from membership of their group. Part Two is for men in positions of pastoral eldership—those who will appoint and care for the house-group leaders. We hope that they will come to Part Two by way of Part One, which will give them an overall view of the way a house group functions and, we trust, answer their questions regarding the viability of house groups in their churches.

Richard and Sue Haydon-Knowell
November 1984

PART ONE

For House-Group Leaders

I

What is a house group?

'I had no qualms at all until ten to eight—then suddenly I realized they would soon be here, and I got jittery! I put a record on to play as people were arriving, then at about twenty past eight I thought, "This is it!", and I switched off the record and welcomed everyone to the group. When I started to speak my whole mouth dried up, I was so nervous.'

'We'd got the children into bed and all the washing-up done by half-past six, so we had time to pray together before people came. I thought I'd be nervous, but I wasn't as bad as Malcolm! When the group got going everybody took part and shared something—it was good.'

'I was relieved that the day had actually arrived—we'd been anticipating it for so long. I was nervous, though, and that meant I spent the early part of the evening in the loo! We wondered whether Lucie would sleep through the evening—Ruth is still breast-feeding her, so we were concerned in case Ruth wouldn't be available all the time. I think it was the realization of the commitment that hit me—we were *committed* to this group of people. It was rather like when we brought Lucie home from the hospital and realized that we were now parents.'

'They were all late arriving—it was twenty-five past eight before everyone was here. I wanted it to go well for Martin, I was really feeling for him! Martin got everyone to introduce themselves, and I suddenly realized that these were *real people* we were to care for—not just a list of names on paper.'

These were the feelings expressed by Malcolm, Janis, Martin and Ruth, two new house-group leaders and their wives, as they spoke about the first meeting of the church house groups for which they had been given responsibility. They had not spent their day in prayer and waiting on God; a holy atmosphere did not prevail in their homes as 8 o'clock approached! Martin teaches in a boys' school and Malcolm is the manager of a large DIY shop. They both had their normal work to do on the day their house groups met for the first time, and their wives had children, babies, housework and meals to cope with.

Most new house-group leaders will readily identify with these four people in their feelings as the evening approached. They knew that the ministers and elders of the church had confidence in them and were praying for them; they knew that God had opened this door of service for them; they had met with the elders for training sessions during the preceding weeks. In spite of all this preparation, when the day came for them to lead their house groups for the first time, they still felt nervous and apprehensive!

We have written this book so that others like Martin and Malcolm may have a reference book to help them in their leadership of church house groups. If you are a house-group leader, or if you aspire to house-group leadership, and want to know how to prepare yourself, or if you are a minister or church leader wanting to know how to use house groups in your church, this book will help you.

What is a house group?

For the purpose of this book, a house group is a group of church members meeting together regularly under the leadership of a man appointed by the minister and elders of the church. The group will normally meet in the leader's home. The group is a pastoral life-function of the church, and its purpose is to bring people to maturity in Christian experience and relationships. It is not a prayer cell, though prayer is a part of house-group life, neither is it a Bible study group, though Bible study may frequently happen on a house-group night.

Not just a 'meeting'

The house group is not just a 'meeting' which happens every week or two; it is a group of people in committed relationship functioning as part of the total life of the church. It is the place where God's people learn how to work out the nitty-gritty of their Christian life. Acts 2:42 speaks of the Christians 'devoting themselves to the apostles' teaching and to the fellowship, to the breaking of bread and to prayer'. The house group is the place where believers who are committed to one another learn together how to apply the teaching of the Scriptures (received each Sunday in church) to their everyday lives. Their commitment to one another enables them to be open with their leader and with each other about their problems, struggles and joys. They learn to pray for each other and to enjoy fellowship on a level which reaches into every area of their lives, not just the 'spiritual'. Learning, sharing, caring, worshipping, praying, socializing—all these things will happen in the house group. God's people are to be a *family*—the New Testament knows nothing of lone or solitary Christians. In a large church there is the danger of someone remaining unnoticed in the crowd, overlooked because he or she is quiet and shy. House groups remove this danger; in the house group everyone is known personally and cared for by a house-group leader who will help each person grow in his relationship with God and with the other people in his group.

How big should a house group be?

The minister and elders of the church will need to come to a decision about the size of house group suitable for their church. This will depend to a certain extent upon the number of house-group leaders available; if the church is setting up house groups for the first time we recommend that leaders are trained and equipped before the house group meetings begin. Some things can only be learnt 'on the job', but proper preparation makes on-the-job learning much easier. (See Part Two of this book for details of selection and training of house-group leaders.) Generally speaking, we feel that house groups work best with between twelve and eighteen members. Fewer than twelve can become a very small meeting if several are absent; more than eighteen is too many for one leader to care for adequately.

Church house groups should never be run on a 'bring-all-your-friends' basis, or their quality and strength will be greatly diluted. There will be times when the house group can be used effectively for planned evangelism (see chapter 6) but the primary purpose of the groups is the bringing of church members to maturity. The groups are *church-based*, and therefore those who come into them should be people who have come into the church under the shepherding care of the minister and elders, to whose leadership the members are committed. It is these leaders who will decide when a house group has grown big enough to be divided or for a few people to be moved from several large groups and put together to form a new group. In our own church, we form a new house group when several groups have reached twenty or more in number, and we aim to be training one or two new leaders before this point is reached, so that there is a leader immediately available. It is good to be constantly prepared for growth! Chapter 11 in Part Two deals with this in more detail.

New wineskins need new wine

In recent years many churches have set up house groups
with varying degrees of success. We must say, in all honesty
and out of many years' involvement with our own and other
churches in the south of England, that the kind of house-
group leadership and life which we are describing in the
following chapters can only happen when the minister,
elders, house-group leaders and church members have experienced the baptism in the Holy Spirit and are walking in
the life, love and commitment to one another which should
flow from this experience. New wineskins need new wine,
and a church which is rigidly traditional or strongly denomi-
national, or where the minister is unwilling to delegate
authority will not benefit from simply applying the 'house-
group formula'. There must be real New Testament life in
the Spirit—a recognition that chapters twelve and fourteen
of the first Corinthian epistle are as vital and relevant as the
oft-quoted chapter thirteen!

Good leadership is vital at all levels

The pastor or minister and elders of a church must lead
lovingly, firmly and biblically, as those who must give
account (Heb 13:17). Authoritarianism has no place in
Scripture, nor should it have any place in the lives of
Christian leaders. Leaders who are committed to the good
of those they lead will deserve and receive their trust and
love. The same applies to house-group leaders, who follow
the example of those over them.

The minister and/or elders should always be 'in touch'
with the house groups and leaders, and no person should be
admitted to a house group without their prior knowledge.
In our own church the elders take the commitment group, a
week in turn; thus they get to know those who are coming
into the church and are able to assess which house group
would be most suitable for them and which house-group

leader could best shepherd them. Even if this cannot be done, there should be constant liaison between pastors and elders and their house-group leaders with regard to the members of the groups.

House groups will not be identical

Each house group, while being part of the church, will have its own identity; and each house-group leader will lead differently according to his own personality and abilities. But certain principles apply to all who are involved in leadership and we will look at these in the following two chapters. In later chapters we shall consider the activities which take place in a house group. In Part Two we shall consider the initial formation of house groups within a church and the relationship of ministers and elders to house-group leaders.

2

The house-group leader

So now you are a house-group leader. Every week your
house group will arrive, looking to you expectantly for
leadership, guidance and help. How does this make you
feel? Glad? Apprehensive? A bit of both? The pressures of
leadership usually reveal the weaknesses in a leader's own
life. In this chapter we shall look at your personal life and
relationships, note the difficulties and problems which may
arise and see how God's provision can meet your areas of
need.

Basic essentials

If you have been appointed to house-group leadership you
will be (or should be!) a man with a foundation of scriptural
truth built into your life; that is, you will have repented of
your sin and been born again through faith in the Lord
Jesus Christ and you will have been baptized in water and in
the Holy Spirit. You will have a basic knowledge of the
truths of God's word, a desire to grow in love for God and
for his people. These basic qualifications are essential. It is
also essential (if you are married) that your wife shares the
same experiences and supports you wholeheartedly, so that
together you can pray and plan for the group in your care.

Your personal relationship with God

As one who is leading others your own personal life and walk with God must be satisfying. Be aware that God cares about you as a person much more than he cares about your success as a house-group leader. Your relationship with God is the most important factor in your life, and will govern the quality of your relationships with your wife, your children, those you lead and the whole family of God. God wants your love before your service, and he wants to pour out his love upon you and make you absolutely secure in him. Indeed, if you are to help your group members to become secure in God, you *must* be secure in God yourself.

Security in God

Security has to do with being consciously rooted, grounded and growing in God. If you have any doubts about your worth in the sight of God, his sovereignty in the circumstances of your birth, parentage, personality and present-day life; if your awareness of personal identity is dependent upon your job status, your qualifications, your achievements or your Christian service; if you feel a need to continually 'prove' or justify yourself to God, others or yourself; if a problem or a pressure situation 'throws' you and you wonder if God is really for you or if he has somehow lost control of your life; or if you are frequently comparing yourself unfavourably with others; then there may be areas of insecurity in your life which will inevitably have an adverse effect on your self-image and on your relationship with the Lord and with his people. Insecurity can also stem from an attitude of unforgiveness towards somebody (perhaps in your past), a lack of real commitment to the purposes of God, a constantly negative attitude towards people or situations, or a failure to feed your mind at the right source, that is, the Scriptures.

The antidote to insecurity

The greatest antidote to personal insecurity is feeding upon, believing and responding to *truth*. The Bible states certain things about you in the following scriptures: Ephesians 1:3–4; 2 Peter 1:1–4; Romans 8:38–39; 1 John 4:16. These scriptures tell you the truth. Believe it! Anything which disagrees with truth is a lie from Satan; you should recognize it as such and reject it. As you feed on the word of God your mind will be renewed to see things from God's perspective, and this will change your negative attitudes. Negative attitudes about people or situations are dangerous. They militate against faith and will damage your leadership. Those in leadership need to be *encouragers*; of themselves first (Ps 42:5) and then of others.

If there is any unforgiveness in your life, any inward reservation about being under authority, or any doubts about God's sovereignty in your life, allow the Holy Spirit to deal with you. Ask him to reveal any areas of insecurity in your life, and the sources of them. Seek God's forgiveness where you have held wrong attitudes, and put matters right with other people where necessary. Respond to God as he reveals things to you, and let his truth bring security into your life.

Commitment

Linked with the matter of security, and equally important, is *commitment*. Firstly, commitment to the Lord Jesus himself who, as Head of the church, has placed you in leadership over your group under the authority of your elders. Does he have the first claim upon your life? Is your love for him growing and increasing, and your fellowship with him growing more intimate? Are you honestly 'seeking first the kingdom of God'? This means desiring above everything else to do the Father's will as Jesus did. It means that his priorities become yours, that your heart beats with his heart, his purpose becomes your vision and his word governs your life.

Commitment to the Lord is also worked out in your commitment to the elders or church leaders who are over you. There may be times when you question their policy in a particular situation; times when you feel they should have acted differently; times when your opinions will differ from theirs. An important aspect of loyalty and commitment is the honest sharing of your opinions with the elders; and a wise eldership will want your insights and comments when they share matters and concerns with you. But if your commitment to them only lasts as long as they are making decisions with which you agree, it is not worth much! The church is not a democracy; God has set elders over his people to govern and lead them in peace and security. The elders who are over you need to be certain of your commitment even when you do not understand or agree with their reasons for a particular decision.

Your commitment must also extend to the group you are leading. They need to know that you really care for them as people, and that you want them to grow into wholeness and maturity. House-group leadership should never be seen as a status symbol (even though you may never actually use that phrase!) but rather as the outworking of a shepherd's heart. People, not programmes, are what matter, and although you will need to plan for and organize your group, the fact that you love them and are committed to them will mean more to them than anything else.

These two matters of security and commitment are vital. There are also other aspects of your relationship with God which are very important. When you become a house-group leader you will not become a mighty Bible expositor overnight! But you will need to learn how to teach basic Bible truth (see chapter 6). You will need to be a man of prayer, able to hear God as you lead and counsel others. For this you will need to grow in your knowledge of the Scriptures and in your faith for God to move in power among the people in your group.

Your spiritual authority

Read the account of the centurion's faith in Luke 7:1–10. Jesus commended this man because of his faith—faith which came as a result of his recognition that Jesus had spiritual authority because of his relationship with God. As a captain of soldiers, appointed by the Emperor and under his authority, he could say to a soldier, 'Do this', and the man would do it. He recognized the same appointment and submission in Jesus, not only in the temporal but in the spiritual and eternal realm.

The same is true of you; if you come into the leadership of a house group it is not because you are self-appointed, but because those in authority have set you there. That means you can pray for, teach and lead those in the group with real authority—not, we hasten to add, authority to rule and 'lord it over' people, but authority to lovingly and wisely protect, provide for and build up those people. See what Paul states as the purpose of authority in 2 Corinthians 10:8. You don't have authority to tell people what colour wallpaper to use, or when to go on holiday, etc, but you do have authority to pray for them, to bring the teaching of Scripture to them and to lead them as a group.

Authority is always a difficult thing to handle. Some people become authoritarian and proud, but the kind of authority that we have been considering is like that of a wise, firm and loving father who seeks the good of the family rather than his own way.

You will find, too, that there is another problem associated with being in a position of leadership. Some people have difficulty in relating to an 'authority figure' of any sort. Either they become silly and unnatural, or they 'clam up' and fail to be as open with you as they might have been were you not in a position of leadership. What is the answer? Certainly it is not to try and be 'one of the boys'! Jesus gives us a beautiful pattern in John 13:13–16. The disciples were right to acknowledge his leadership and he exercised his leadership to serve them. He was both their leader and their friend (Jn 13:13; 15:15). You must seek grace to be the same.

You will find that now you are a leader, people will look to you to lead. The group will make demands upon you, and you may find yourself thinking, 'What am I doing here?' There will be times when you will want to do what Saul did when he was chosen for leadership—hide among the baggage (1 Sam 10:21–22). Don't do it! Believe that God, through your leaders and elders, has given you authority to lead and care for the group. If you are young, take special note of 1 Timothy 4:12–16.

You are accountable

Remember that your authority in the house group is delegated authority. You are accountable to the minister and/ or elders of your church. This means that you will not seek to keep your house group to yourself or see yourself as ruling over a 'little kingdom', but rather that you will recognize yourself to be a 'servant' of the eldership. Important decisions regarding the members of the house group, or particular problems concerning individuals, should be shared and discussed with the elders when you meet with them (as you should do on a regular basis) to discuss the progress of your group.

Accountability also means that *you* will be shepherded and cared for by those to whom you are accountable. Very often you will be hearing and dealing with the problems of the people in your group, and you will be tested and stretched spiritually and emotionally. You need a shepherd who will care for you and your wife, who will minister to you and build you up. Your minister or one of your elders should be designated for this, so that you do not carry your responsibilities without help and guidance. You and your wife must be willing and open to share personal difficulties and problems which affect you, your family or your ministry. Failure to be open with those who care for you will prevent you receiving help when you need it, which will in turn adversely affect your care of your house group. God's people, whether shepherds or sheep, were never intended to bear burdens alone!

Pressures that come with leadership

Leadership, even of such a small number as a house group, will bring certain pressures which would not come in the ordinary way. We shall now look at some of these.

Satan will single you out for attack

Have you ever noticed that if there are upheavals in the family they will come on a Sunday more often than not, or that the baby is fretful and won't sleep when there is a meeting in the home? We should not be surprised at this; we have an enemy who knows when he can cause the most damage. You and your wife will find that the enemy will seek to attack you much more as you come into leadership. God will even permit this so that you may learn to depend on him. Paul was not unaware of Satan's schemes (2 Cor 2:11), nor why difficulties came (2 Cor 1:9). It is as well for us to be aware of how he works. Don't be surprised if you and your wife come under attack or find that your relationship with each other is tested (especially on the day of the house group!) Stand your ground and don't let the enemy overcome you.

Don't let Satan bring you into condemnation

Another way Satan will seek to attack you is to bring you into condemnation. There will be times when you will make mistakes, times when you realize that your leadership is not always received gladly, times when you realize you have given someone the wrong counsel. There may be times when you fall into sin, quarrel with your wife, shout at your children or slam the door on the cat. At times like these, Satan will come to you as the 'accuser of the brethren' (Rev 12:10). 'Great house-group leader *you* are! If the group could only have heard you just now! And if the elders had any idea how you handled that situation they wouldn't keep you in leadership a day longer. God can't overlook this sort of thing—better resign now before they throw you out!'

If you begin to believe the accusations of Satan he will immediately bring you into condemnation. As someone has said, 'Satan not only knocks you down—he puts the boot in as well!' Learn to recognize his accusations. Anything which causes you to feel shamed, degraded and rejected is from the enemy; it is *not* the conviction of the Holy Spirit. The Holy Spirit does indeed convict us of sin, but he is gentle with us and seeks to produce in us 'a repentance that leads to salvation and leaves no regret' (2 Cor 7:10). Satan's accusations are designed to leave us feeling hopeless, condemned and totally unworthy. If he succeeds, you are effectively rendered useless and joyless.

Recognize that if you are to lead your group in freedom and joy you *must* resist Satan in this area of condemnation. Do not listen when he tells you that you have no right to a close relationship with God; that the sin you committed last week cannot be forgotten by God or you until next month, even though it has been forgiven; that you are not an up-to-standard Christian (let alone an up-to-standard house-group leader) so you cannot really expect God to answer when you pray. Stand against this sort of thing with the truth of God.

Revelation 12:11 tells us that Satan is overcome by 'the blood of the lamb' and 'the word of testimony'. You are justified before God through the blood of Jesus which was poured out for you when he died on the cross. That *alone* brings you into relationship with God; it is nothing to do with your ability, worth or effort. Your sins (past and present) are forgiven because Jesus died for you—not because you atone for them by good behaviour after you have been forgiven. When Satan brings accusations against

you, reaffirm what God says about you in passages like
Romans 5:1–11, and refuse the accusations of your enemy
who is a liar (Jn 8:44), a thief and a destroyer
(Jn 10:10). Realize that his aim is to destroy you and thus
attack your house group. Realize also that he was totally
conquered and shown up through the death of Jesus on the
cross (Col 2:13–15). Enter into that victory!

Pressure of being in the public eye

The simple fact of having responsibility can itself become a
pressure. This is especially true if you are young or in-
experienced in a leadership role. The verses referred to
earlier in 1 Timothy 4:12–16 have some appropriate counsel.

Pressure to 'make it'

It is quite common to discover that in any group of leaders
everyone feels that every other person's group is better,
bigger, more successful, more spiritual, etc, than his own!
The other groups are all running smoothly—yours is the
only one with problems! You can either react by feeling
utterly dejected or by trying to match or even to cap what
another leader may have just shared in a leadership meeting. Let's be clear about this: we are not in some competition to have the best, biggest, most spiritual group. You
will need to learn to be at peace in your heart and to rejoice
at the good progress of other leaders.

Secondly, you will need to learn to give an honest report
of the way your group is going, neither exaggerating nor
concealing the truth.

Thirdly, you need to recognize that both you and your
group will be different from other leaders and other groups.
Leaders and groups have their own individual identities!

Fourthly, you will need to set realistic goals for yourself
and your group rather than trying to compete with others.

Lastly, don't try and function beyond your ability. You
are yourself, and you need to function at the level where
God has placed you.

Pressure of time

Both you and your wife are going to have to plan for the extra commitments that house-group leadership will bring. You will need to sit down with your wife and establish a 'plan of campaign', bearing in mind the importance of having time on your own together and, of course, time with your family. Make sure your children don't feel 'pushed out' by the new and larger family of the house-group. The best way is to plan that Monday night, say, is your 'family night'. Make this known to the group so that you are not disturbed by visits or phone calls on that evening. Plan in some times of 'switching off' with a hobby or relaxation. There will be occasions when you have to say 'no' to the demands of people in the group because of family calls upon your time. You should not feel guilty about this: if there is a good relationship of love between you and the members of your group they will know that you will be in contact as soon as possible to help with their problem.

Your relationship with your wife

In a survey of house-group leaders where the question was asked, 'What is the most important factor in your ministry?', by far the largest number said it was their relationship with their wives. When you think about it, that is not surprising. God has joined you to each other to become one, and therefore your relationship is of the utmost importance. Keeping certain things in mind will help to maintain a good relationship.

Recognize your differing roles

House-group leadership is not a joint leadership in which you both have an equal role. The husband is the leader and is, as such, answerable to the eldership. The wife is in a supportive role and does not have the same independent leadership responsibility. That means she should be safeguarded from coming under the direct pressure of leadership. Decisions regarding the group may at times be taken jointly, but the responsibility must always be the husband's. However, as most men will know, although the wife's role is supportive, it is absolutely invaluable. Learn to listen to your wife; she will have insight and understanding (especially of other women) which can be of great help. Her more warm, responsive and compassionate woman's nature will need, at times, to be balanced by your more objective assessments, but you will find that her insights are often on target. Learn how to receive from one another in this way.

Your wife, too, will be the key factor in making people feel at home, organizing refreshments, making sure there is a cake when it is somebody's birthday; going out in friendship to new people, etc. Some wives will be accustomed to entertaining; for others it will be a new experience, and your encouragement will be needed and appreciated.

Pray, share and plan together

Communication is vital. (This does not just apply to housegroup matters!) It would be easy to plan the house group evening on your own, and when they all pour in through the front door to announce, 'Tonight we're going to have refreshments first, followed by a Bible study!', leaving your puzzled and slightly harassed wife to wonder why you didn't tell her earlier. However used you may have been to doing things on your own in the past, you will need now to learn to plan and then to share and pray with your wife about the evening.

Whether you lead a house group or not, it is God's will for you and your wife to pray together. See how this is mentioned in the Scriptures as the normal practice for Christian husbands and wives in 1 Peter 3:7. Learn to share what God shows you from the Scriptures so that you build each other up in the Lord.

In every area of your life be aware of each other's needs; don't deprive each other sexually (1 Cor 7:3–5). If you see that your wife is getting under pressure from the children, housework, etc, don't neglect it but help lift the load. Take care of each other. Learn to communicate meaningfully. Share one another's interests.

Remember that some members of your house group (particularly young people who are new Christians) may never have been in a Christian home before, and you and your wife will be the first example of a Christian marriage they meet at close quarters. Many young people (and older ones too) come from homes where there has been a break-up of their parents' marriage or where the relationship is stormy and unhappy. To be welcomed into a Christian home and to see an open and loving Christian marriage will be as much a part of your ministry to them as the teaching you give them in the house group on Wednesday evenings. No marriage is perfect, and you will not want the people in your group to think that you and your wife never have problems, but as they see you facing and dealing with your family difficulties in a loving and biblical way, they will learn how Christian relationships are worked out and their confidence in your leadership will increase.

3

The house-group leader's wife

Wednesday nights will be different now! You and your husband may be used to entertaining friends for meals, coffee or just chat. But you have always invited them on a date convenient to you, and you have always chosen specific people. Now a large group of people will descend on your front room every house-group evening, and you and your husband will not only be responsible for looking after them then but also for building them up spiritually and teaching them how to apply the truth of Scripture in a practical way to their own lives. And *you* haven't even chosen them! This particular group of people has been chosen by the elders to come into your care. You may not even *like* some of them! Added to which, your husband is going to be leading them each house-group evening, and how will he shape up? Will you sit there mentally biting your fingernails as he tries to cope with awkward questions and theological red herrings? As time passes and the group begins to have confidence in your husband's leadership (and thus to come to him for help and counsel) will you begin to feel left out, or that you are in competition with the group for your husband's time and interest? (He's been promising for weeks to paint the kitchen cupboards, but one of the group is having a really hard time at work and needs to come and chat about it tonight....)

28

Your needs

Your basic needs are exactly the same as those of your husband, and we suggest that you read through the sections in the previous chapter dealing with 'Your personal relationship with God' and 'Security in God'. All this applies to you as well! Your husband should also read this chapter, particularly the sections on 'Communication'.

Your self-image

Your self-image is very important. We spoke in the previous chapter about the need for men in leadership to avoid unhelpful comparisons of themselves with other leaders. The same is true of leaders' wives. A good self-image and an acceptance of yourself will prevent this kind of comparison.

Learn to be yourself; God created you with the kind of personality he wanted you to have. He gave you particular abilities and gifts, and he wants you to reach your potential in those things, not to spend your time trying to copy someone else or to be what you think someone else would prefer. Feelings of fear and inadequacy (which adversely affect your self-image) often spring from the pressure of trying to conform to an unreal standard; you may have been subjected to demands and expectations in childhood which have left you feeling that you must behave in a certain way in order to 'make the grade'. Possibly you feel that a leader's wife should be a special kind of person. You are not that kind of person, so perhaps you feel that you must do your best to *become* that kind of person? If this is the case, your mind needs to be renewed through the word of God. You need to be deeply assured of God's love for you *as you are,* especially if you have been deceived into thinking that the pressures of your unreal standard have come from him. God never wills this kind of pressure for us—his will is 'good, pleasing and perfect' (Rom 12:2).

Enjoy being yourself. Make the most of your appearance and discover what kind of clothes and make-up suit you. Don't copy others or feel that you have to follow any other 'style' than that which is right for you in matters of dress, diet or anything else. Jesus sets you free to be *you*, and he will let you know if he wants to change anything!

Work at necessary tasks until you are efficient. Cooking may not be your greatest talent, but if your husband is in leadership you will need to entertain. Practise two or three menus until you are confident and proficient. Establish your talents; find out what you are good at and develop it. You may discover that you are very good at gardening or pottery or Portuguese! Your skills can be enjoyed by your friends and the members of your house group; be ready to teach others what you have learned, and to receive the things that they can teach you. Recognizing the fact that your talents can benefit other people is a great help to your self-image.

Talk honestly with your husband about your priorities and abilities; ask him to be specific about the ways in which he expects you to support his leadership. Bear in mind that life moves on in stages; your priorities and commitments will need to be reviewed every so often. Nappies and teething do not go on for ever (it only seems like it!), babies grow into toddlers who eventually reach school age. But at whatever stage you are, it is vital that your self-image is a positive one if you are to function well as a leader's wife.

Your role

Your role is not that of a joint house-group leader! That authority and responsibility is your husband's. Your role is to support his ministry, serving alongside him in building up and caring for the house group. At times this will mean being with him to bring counsel and encouragement to someone with a problem, or to a couple who want help in their marriage or advice about handling their children. If a girl or woman in your group needs counsel your husband may want you to talk with her; if he decides to talk with her himself he may want you to be present. (There are times when it is inadvisable for a house-group leader to counsel a member of the opposite sex on his own; a single house-group leader should ask a trusted Christian woman to be present in these situations.) Recognize that the 'difficult' people, the ones who demand attention frequently and always seem to be in trouble, are those with deep needs in their lives. Consistent care, love and teaching from your husband and yourself, together with the on-going teaching and life of the church, will help them to become more balanced; they will learn to hear God for themselves and to see his answers to their problems. Be committed to this ministry of support, so that your husband does not have the added pressure of you 'competing' with the house group for his time and attention. He, in turn, must be aware of your needs and the times when the priorities of family life will require him to say 'no' to demands from people in the group.

We dealt with the matter of commitment to your church leaders in the previous chapter, and it is important for you to share your husband's commitment to those over you in God. But for you, commitment to your husband is something vitally important in marriage, quite apart from the house group! You need to really *know* your husband; know how to communicate with him, how to support him and back him up, how to encourage him when group leadership brings pressures upon him. The next section will help you to see ways of improving your marriage communication.

Your relationships

Your relationship with Jesus is the most important factor in your life. You need to make time in your routine to read the Scriptures and spend time with the Lord developing your relationship with him, learning from him and enjoying fellowship with him. You will find some suggestions about this in the chapters 'Teaching in the house group' and 'Praying in the house group'.

Second only to your relationship with the Lord is your relationship with your husband, who has the next claim on your time and attention. Never forget that the role of 'wife' has priority over the role of 'mother'. If your children know that Daddy is 'Number One' in your life it will bring them great security. Your relationship with your children is your next priority, followed by the running of your home to provide a secure and peaceful base for your family. Then comes your relationship with the group which has been given into your care.

Leadership pressures often reveal the weaknesses in a marriage; be prepared to work at your relationship with your husband for your own sakes as well as for the sake of your house group. There are some excellent books available on Christian marriage; we particularly recommend *Strike the Original Match* by Charles Swindoll, *How to be Happy Though Married* by Tim LaHaye, and *The Act of Marriage* (dealing with the sexual side of marriage) by Tim and Beverly LaHaye. Another helpful little book is *Marriage in the Balance* by Ann Warren. These books will also be helpful to you in your leadership of the house group should you need to talk to anyone in the group about marriage difficulties. You may have more time and inclination than your husband to read books; but he will be open to talk when you share with him what you have learned, and both of you will benefit.

Communication—with your husband

Good communication is vital to the development of a good relationship. Learn to improve communication with your husband. Be sensitive to his needs and let him know that he can totally depend upon your love and support both in his headship of your family and in his leadership of the house group. A few 'don'ts' may be helpful here!

Don't criticize or judge your husband's 'style' because it is different from yours (or different from that of Mavis's husband, or Dorothy's husband.... Accept him as God's choice for you and as the one to whom God has joined you in order to complete both of you. Pray for your husband and thank God for him every day, and ask God to make you really appreciative of his good points. You should not try to manipulate or organize your husband. God has made him head over you and your family, and he will never progress in that role (nor in his capacity as a leader), if you are constantly attempting to control his time or his actions. Learn to trust your husband; the Holy Spirit will teach him as you release him.

Don't let the 'silent resentment syndrome' destroy your relationship with your husband. Resentment is sin, and needs to be confessed and forgiven; it is also a barrier to communication because of the emotional reactions it produces when it finally surfaces. If a pressure or a problem arises in your relationship ask the Holy Spirit to enable you to share any grievance against your husband with him in a way that does not either blame him or demoralize him. Bear in mind that the hurt may be entirely unintentional; he may be totally unaware of having hurt you! Bear in mind, too, that there may be areas where you have hurt or offended him. Learning to verbalize your feelings and your expectations of one another will help you to come to a greater degree of mutual understanding. Husbands are notoriously bad thought-readers; waiting for him to 'know how you feel' *without telling him* is a non-starter!

Don't forget that timing is an important element in communication. It is not wise to unload your problems the moment your husband arrives home—even if you have had a terrible day! Give him a few minutes to unwind from the pressures of his own day; then he will be able to involve himself much more readily in your situation. Remember, too, that men are far more single-minded than women, and cannot easily cope with several matters at the same time;

therefore it is unwise to attempt a serious discussion with him during *Match of the Day* or *Tomorrow's World*. Agree with him to talk before or after the programme (or whatever else is demanding his attention) at a time when you can both give yourselves to the matter under discussion. It is important to make time for talking urgent matters over, even if it means leaving the baby with a neighbour and locking the other children in the back garden for half an hour!

Manner, as well as timing, is important. If you communicate with your husband in a very loud and dominant fashion, or if you frequently resort to tears and tantrums, he will probably 'switch off'. God commands you to respect your husband (Eph 5:33). Be especially careful at certain times of the month or when you are otherwise under pressure.

Don't practise 'resurrection ministry' on an issue which has been talked over, settled and closed. Husbands call this *nagging*! If your husband, after discussing a matter with you and hearing your opinions, makes a decision which you do not agree with you must honour him as your head and respect that decision.

After the 'don'ts', the 'do's'! Remember that sex is a vitally important part of communication in marriage. Enjoy it! Improving your relationship in this area will be a means of relaxing and blessing you both. We recommend the book mentioned above, *The Act of Marriage*. We also strongly recommend fitting a lock on your bedroom door! Children need to learn from an early age that there are times when Mummy and Daddy want to be alone together, although clearly you should aim to have such times when toddlers are asleep.

Seek help if there are areas where you and your husband find it hard to communicate, or if you are not meeting one another's needs except on a superficial level. Go together to your pastor or minister, or to another leader you can trust, and be open with him about your difficulties. It is vitally important that husbands and wives who are in leadership should be absolutely at one, able to trust one another and to communicate on all levels.

Communication—with your children

Improving your communication with your husband will help you to improve your communication with your children. Teach your children to look to him as head of the family and to recognize his authority and leadership under God. Let him handle any serious disputes among the children and be ultimately responsible for disciplining them, even though you will be the one who copes more often with the day-to-day discipline.

You will already be teaching your children what it means to be a Christian. Teach them also to trust God's provision for you as a family and to expect him to answer prayer.

Be as polite to your children as you would be to a visitor in your home. (Your children are more important than your visitors!) Your children learn communication from you; if you shout at them, nag them or ignore them they will behave in the same way to each other and to the boy next door. Realize, too, that you communicate to your children *what you really are*; if you are less than honest in your relationships (for example, friendly and committed to someone in public, but critical of him in your home) the same attitudes will be reproduced in your children.

Recognize that your children are not just small extensions of you and your husband; they are individuals with hearts, minds and personalities of their own. Learn to listen to them and try to understand their points of view. Be aware of their individual emotional needs. Look back on your own emotional needs during childhood and teens; this will help you to identify and meet those same needs in your children. If your own needs were *not* adequately met, you may need help in seeing how to deal with your children and teenagers. Talk with other Christian parents who are handling their children well and take advantage of the many helpful books available. We particularly recommend two books by Dr James Dobson, *Dare to Discipline* and *Hide or*

Seek for guidance and help with your toddlers and younger children. Another title by James Dobson, *Preparing for Adolescence,* is a most helpful book for parents to read and then pass on to their children from the age of about twelve years. A helpful book to give older teenagers is *Givers, Takers and Other Kinds of Lovers* by Josh McDowell. Never build your life totally around your children or let them rule and dominate your existence; this is neither good for them nor for you. (A possessive mother may damage a child emotionally.)

Pray constantly for your children, building open and friendly relationships with them as they grow older. Recognize the fact that (eventually!) you must let your children go. As they reach their late teen years you can begin to help them prepare to 'leave the nest'. Teach them to look forward with joy and anticipation to the future God has for them. Equip them as much as possible for independent life in ways such as teaching them to handle money, teaching them to cook and cope with household duties. Encourage them to be considerate and help others.

It is never wise to criticize or judge your teenage children, or try to force them into your own mould. Maintain a relaxed and open attitude toward them, and keep your home and your heart open to their friends. If your teenager should turn away from the things of God, maintain a loving relationship while making it clear that he must respect the rules of a Christian home. Share your teenager's need with others who can pray with you. Be aware that God wants to teach and mould *you* through the pain of this situation. Weep before God, not before your teenager.

Don't feel hurt if your Christian teenagers sometimes turn to other Christians for help and encouragement rather than to you. They are not rejecting *you*; it is simply that at this time in their lives it is easier to share with someone other than family—someone who is able to view their problems more objectively than an emotionally involved parent. Be glad that your teenager trusts your brothers and sisters in Christ enough to turn to them for help. (*Their* children will probably come to *you*!)

Communication—with those you lead

When you are in leadership it is important to be open and honest with those you lead. Be real in your communication; don't give the impression that you have 'arrived' in every area, but be honest about your own difficulties—at the same time encouraging others who are facing problems to believe God as you do for eventual victory. As you and your husband grow in God, be prepared to share with others and to lead them into the same experience of truth.

Don't communicate in a way which brings people under pressure. (For instance, as you pass a friend taking the children to school, don't say, 'Hi, Jane! I've managed to fit in my ironing before coming out this morning as well as baking a couple of cakes! And guess what? On the way down I witnessed to three neighbours! How have *you* got on?') When you are beginning to build a relationship with someone, keep your communication low-key. As the relationship grows and trust develops, your communication can reach a deeper level.

Another vital lesson for those in a position of leadership is to learn to love. God is willing to teach you how to love if you are willing to learn; this is clear from 1 Thessalonians 3:12 and 4:9. Learning to love means getting to *know* a person. Invite someone to your home for a day; this is especially helpful for younger wives and mums with whom you can share recipes, homemaking ideas and help with children as well as spiritual truth and encouragement in the things of God. Others may be able to come for an evening meal, or at some other time. As you spend time with people, learn what their interests are and how they live their lives. Ask God for understanding of their needs, and be prepared to share yourself with them.

Have patience with people; you should expect growth, but not necessarily by next Thursday! When your husband

or you have to bring correction or guidance to someone in
your group, do it with love and understanding; don't pull
the person down or cause him or her to despair—authority
is not for that purpose (2 Cor 13:10). Encourage the person
to grow in maturity and come into victory in the weak area.
Reassure the person with a problem that God *does* have an
answer and that together you will seek him for it. If a matter
(particularly one involving relationships) cannot be solved
quickly, be prepared to set short-term goals towards which
the person can work.

Your lifestyle

When you come into leadership your life becomes busier!
You have all the family and household chores to cope with,
but you now have the added responsibility of sharing in the
care of (and thus being involved with) a large number of
other people who will want your company and your attention. If you are not to become emotionally drained by the
task you need to organize your life in such a way that you
will be 'on top' or even 'one jump ahead' of all the demands
which are made upon you. You only have twenty-four
hours in each day, and if those hours are not spent wisely
you will come under pressure. It is important to recognize
that you cannot say 'yes' to every claim upon your time.
You need to find *God's priorities* for your life; and when
you bring your priorities into line with his, your life will
come into peace and order.

Relationships with people in the house group will flow
out of your husband's leadership ministry. Often this will
involve your children and home as you share your life with
those in your care. But be watchful in this area; some
involvements may not be the will of God—they may be the
will of someone in the house group who is anxious to
monopolize your time and attention. Mistaken or misguided
involvement can be emotionally taxing and can rob your
family of your time and energy. Be guided by your husband

in this; discuss together the degree of involvement that you as a leader's wife can have without your personal and family life coming under pressure. God is sovereign—he does not have to use *you* to help every person in your patch. You will always have time and energy for those whom God brings specifically to you, and he will enable you to say 'no' to others without feeling condemned or hurtful.

Organizing your time

Stand back and have a good look at the way you organize your week. Some hours are fixed (school attendance, clinic days, working hours if you are in full- or part-time employment), but much of your time is in your control. Ask yourself if there are certain days in the week when you are under pressure, or if there are areas of household or child management where you could find more efficient ways of doing things.

Be aware of the times when a crisis is likely to arise. Sunday morning, when you are trying to get the family ready for church and prepare lunch at the same time? Weekdays at 6 p.m., when baby needs a feed, three-year-old is fretful, eight-year-old needs help with his homework and husband is about to arrive home for the evening meal which you have not yet cooked? Efficient preparation can help to avert crises. Peel the potatoes on Saturday night, and lay the table for Sunday lunch immediately breakfast is cleared away. (All the cutlery and glasses, etc., required for Sunday lunch can be stacked on a tray Saturday night.) Cook items like apple pie or Yorkshire pudding during the week and freeze them ready for Sunday. Perhaps your husband would prepare breakfast for the family on Sunday morning to free you for organizing lunch?

On weekdays do as much preparation as possible for the evening meal after breakfast; you can peel the potatoes, cut up the meat and prepare the pudding. If you can, spend one whole day a month baking and freeze the results. This will save you being caught out for time to bake when the children go down with measles or your husband decides to take a few days off. Arrange to have fish and chips or a Chinese take-away for the evening meal on your busiest weekday (house-group day?).

Every day, make sure you sit down for a short break at intervals; this may coincide with play school or nap-time if you have toddlers. You will get through more work by taking more rest! The will of God for you includes rest and recreation, and if you are always tired and working against time there is certainly a need (after checking that there is nothing physically wrong) for some re-organization of your time. You need some time in each day to 'be yourself', to relax and choose what you will do—even if it is only to read a thriller for half an hour or to play a favourite record. Hobbies like knitting or patchwork are relaxing and can be picked up at any time. When babies and toddlers are occupying most of your time it is important to keep your mind active rather than becoming submerged in feeding, potty-training and teething, important (and fascinating!) as these things are.

Examine your methods of work. Are you spending too much time on non-essentials—polishing the rubber-plant, ironing the underwear? Make a plan of your week's work, listing the jobs. Now make another plan, spreading the week's work over a fortnight. (Obviously this cannot apply to everything, especially if you have small children. But there are plenty of chores which can be done every other week. No one will die of shock; they probably won't even notice!)

You may find it helpful to compile a 'Useful Book'. Buy a large, lined, hard-covered exercise book and divide it into sections. Use one section for a list of birthdays you need to remember, a page for each month. Use one section as a menu list; write down the names of folk who visit your home for a meal, together with the date and details of the meal. Not only will this eventually become a useful menu list, it will also ensure that you do not serve people the same

meal twice! Use another section for Christmas details—card
list, present list, shopping list for Christmas food, party
games, etc. Keep another section for holiday lists; jobs to
be done before you leave (who will feed the cat?), clothes
list, food list, camping gear list, children's toy list. Make
one section a shopping check list; write down every item in
your cupboards, fridge and freezer—then all you need to
do on shopping days is go through your list and jot down the
items you need. Have a section for large-number catering
(e.g. house-group meal). Write down the menu and an
itemized shopping list with prices; you will find it invaluable
next time. Use one page of your book as a 'husband's job
list', so that when he says, 'Is there anything you'd like me
to do, darling?', you can immediately reply, 'Yes, love, put
another screw in the bathroom towel-rail', instead of standing speechless! Other ideas for your 'Useful Book' will
occur to you according to your life-style, and you will have
your information to hand whenever you need it. You will
also find it helpful to have a small notebook as an 'action
book' to use in conjunction with the larger book. This is for
shopping lists, lists of jobs for the day, reminders, etc.

  Learn from your friends. If someone has a quick way of
doing a job, adopt it. If someone is especially efficient in a
certain area, ask her for some hints. Learn to share ideas
and needs; at times you will be asking for help, at other
times you will be giving it.

  If you have babies or small children you need the friendship and strengthening of others in a similar situation. If
your church fellowship has a large group of young mums, it
can be helpful to divide into smaller groups to share baby-
minding. With a group of three mums, each one can take it
in turns to have all the children one morning a week. This
method can be adapted in various ways, but it gives everyone
a break (babies and toddlers included!). With playgroup or
school-age children it can be used during the holidays. It is
also a good idea to have a lunchtime date with another
mum at least once a week and to entertain someone yourself

for lunch once in the week—this is good for both mums and small children.

Teach your children to do small jobs while they are young. Even pre-schoolers can learn to lay the table and clear things away (don't use your best china while they are at this stage) and also to pick up their toys. Assess the abilities of your child as he grows and give him jobs within his capabilities.

Choosing wisely

'What do you do with your spare time?' may seem a purely academic question to someone who is coping with a home, a young family *and* a house group! You may have only a very limited amount of time to yourself, particularly when your children are small. But limited time makes right choices even more important; however large or small the amount of time you have, your choices are vital; *they help to determine what you will become.* In the previous section we saw the need for rest and recreation, and for time to 'be yourself'. In Philippians 4:8 there is clear direction for any decisions we make about ways of using our time when we have a choice.

As a child of the King you need to feed your mind at the right source. This means reading and understanding the Scriptures. Christian books can be helpful, too, especially biographies and practical books on prayer, Christian living, etc. When you read secular books, especially fiction, make Philippians 4:8 your criterion; this will mean that there will be many authors whose books will never reach your shelves. It is worth spending the time to find fiction authors whose books are clean and enjoyable, especially if you have teenage children who will need guidance in their own reading. The fact that you are in leadership will also mean that members of your house group (particularly the young people) will look to you for guidance in this area. Ration your reading of women's magazines; reading too many can give you an 'escapist' mentality, as can unrestricted reading of fiction. Teach your children to enjoy books, and introduce them early to the public library.

Television will feed your mind, but not always with the right food! Again, make Philippians 4:8 the measure of your viewing. You may have to turn the TV set off frequently (or not switch it on!) and be prepared to explain your reasons. The same applies if you enjoy listening to music; you will need to exercise care in your choices. Much of today's pop music, especially heavy rock, is satanic in origin and can only have a bad effect on you.

Avoid negative and unhelpful friendships. This does not mean you should not cultivate non-Christian friends, but their influence should not be a strong factor in your life. If you spend time with negative or unhelpful Christians (and in leadership you will probably have to do so some of the time, unless you have a perfect house group!), seek to remain firmly positive and help them to a more scriptural standpoint. Cultivate positive friendships where you can encourage one another in God while enjoying activities together. Check out your interests; some hobbies can be harmful to your spiritual life. Jogging is fine, yoga is definitely not! Its roots are in Hinduism and it is dangerous to think it can so easily be divorced from its roots. Keeping physically fit is important and enjoyable. You can do it at home, using an exercise routine such as the Health Education Council 'Looking After Yourself' chart, or go to a Keep Fit class (many of the Adult Education Institutes have crèche facilities) or, if you are brave enough, jog in your local park. If four mums go together, two of you can look after the children while two of you jog round the park; then change places. Once you have made the effort to begin you will find exercising beneficial and relaxing.

Check that your diet is a sensible one, for your own and your family's sake. A good book on nutrition will help you to know which foods are good and which are to be avoided. If you are overweight, the 'Looking After Yourself' booklet from the Health Education Council (mentioned above) will show you how to diet sensibly and to lose weight slowly and consistently rather than attempting crash diets which often result in an equally rapid weight gain afterwards.

Look carefully at all these suggestions and ask God if he wants any of them put into action in your life, both to glorify him and to help you become a more relaxed and efficient house-group leader's wife—which will glorify him anyway!

4

Getting off the ground

In this chapter we shall consider your first house-group meeting. We shall think about some of the practical considerations which ensure the smooth running of the group, and we shall look at the long-term aims and goals of the group.

That first evening

The first meeting of your house group, as far as you the leader are concerned, does not start at 8 p.m. on a particular evening. It starts well before then, as you meet with your pastor and elders for training sessions and as you pray for those who will be in your group. You will begin by asking God to show you how to spend that first evening together. As you and your wife plan and pray the evening will take shape in your mind.

The room where the group will meet needs to be tidy and have enough seating for everybody. Floor cushions are useful if you do not have enough chairs; these are easily made at home if you do not want to go to the expense of buying them. Beach and garden chairs can also be used—anything on which people can sit comfortably for a couple of hours. Make the room as welcoming as you can; have a fire on if the weather is cold. A record or tape playing quietly in the background is pleasant as people arrive.

Be ready, with your wife, to welcome people when they start arriving. Make sure there is somewhere to hang or put their coats, and let them know where the toilet is (especially if you plan to serve coffee at the beginning of the evening!). Introduce people individually if they do not already know one another. Ask them what sort of day they have had, and tell them about yours. Make them feel at home, and let them know that you are interested in them. Let the shy ones sit in quiet corners if they want to, but make sure that you have welcomed them and 'made contact' in a definite way.

Allow people to chat together for twenty minutes or so, by which time even the late ones should have arrived. Then switch off the record player and welcome everyone to the first meeting of the group. You may want to start by committing the evening to God in prayer; this could be followed by everyone in the group giving his or her name and some personal information. Following this you may, as leader of the group, want to speak about the aims and goals of the group and the things you will do together in the coming weeks. This could be followed by a time of worshipping the Lord together, after which coffee could be served.

This is one possible pattern for your first meeting, but you may want to vary it. You may decide to start with a buffet meal together, with a time of sharing afterwards; or a time of sharing and prayer followed by communion—breaking bread and drinking wine together as Jesus commanded his followers to do.

At the end of the evening you may feel that it has not gone as well as you expected or hoped, but this should not discourage you. You do not have to hit some sort of 'jackpot' the first evening—or any evening for that matter! House-group leadership is an ongoing commitment. In six months' time ask yourself and your group if they are feeling cared-for as individuals.

More practical details

Some practical details will need attention every week. Perhaps initially your wife could make the coffee, but eventually it would be a good thing to have a rota, so that your wife can remain in the room and be available to people. Let the group get acquainted with your kitchen (it doesn't have to be spotless) so that they know where to find coffee, biscuits, etc. You may like to have a rota for someone to bake a cake each week, if you prefer something more than biscuits. It is good to have a special cake if it is somebody's birthday; keep a list of birthdays so that everyone receives a card from the group on the nearest house-group evening. (In our own church, many of the house groups have their own highly individual rendering of 'Happy Birthday to You'!) Birthday-cake baking and the compiling of a birthday list are matters which can be delegated to someone in the group who is willing and happy to take them on.

If you have small children, you will want to have them in bed (and preferably asleep) by the time your house group arrives, and this may mean helping your wife with washing-up and bedtime chores, if you don't already do this. Older children need to be settled happily in another room while the house group is taking place. As we said earlier, make sure your children do not feel 'pushed out' by the house group. They may be used to Dad being out on some evenings, or Mum being out on some evenings, but now both Mum and Dad (and the front room!) will be unavailable one evening *every* week. Talk to your children about the house group, let them get to know the people in the group, and make sure that they do not feel that it is taking your love and concern away from them.

Goals and aims

A house group is people—who will come pouring through your front door every house-group night indefinitely. They will soon begin to form an identity as a group, and relationships will begin to grow. Your aim is *to bring those people to maturity*. But what exactly does this mean, and how will you go about it?

In Colossians 1:28 Paul speaks of 'admonishing and teaching everyone with all wisdom, so that we may present everyone perfect in Christ'. The word 'perfect' in the Greek is *teleios*, which signifies 'having reached its end' or become mature, fully grown, complete. It is evident from Paul's comment in verse 29 that people do not just become mature automatically.

Let us consider an imaginary house group of a dozen people. There are Bill and Helen Square, who have been traditionalists most of their converted lives, never saying very much in the church; they are now in their fifties, have just been baptized in the Spirit and are poised to leap forward or settle back into the old rut. Heather Novel and Jill Springer are both at art college, bristling with ideas, thrilled at all God is doing and longing to see the whole world saved next week! Bob New is in his teens and just converted. He has heard of Matthew, Mark, Luke and John but wonders who on earth Deuteronomy is. Paul and Pam Sore are both divorcees, converted two years ago after marrying each other; both are still suffering from the scars of their previous disastrous marriages. They have four children between them. John Bright is in his late twenties, an industrial chemist; he plays the guitar, reads a lot of solid Christian books and was brought up in a fine Christian home. Brian and Pat Good are in their thirties with three young children; they have a lovely marriage, though Pat is inclined to dominate and is working hard at submission. Robert Old is a retired widower, knows the Bible inside out, but is not too clear what's happening in the church—only that God must be in it all, as there has never been such growth before. Janet Sharp is a school-teacher (maths) of some fifteen years standing, well taught, baptized in the Spirit seven years ago. Very loyal and committed but just a little intolerant of people who are slow or cannot come through problems.

Before we look in more detail at this goal of bringing people to maturity, consider this imaginary group of people and write down those obvious and immediate areas of need in which each individual is going to require help if he is going to come to maturity in Christ. You will see at once that there can be no single approach to all these areas of need. The reason is that maturity is not the result of growth in just one or two segments of our lives, *but in the whole*. A tree is a good example of this—it grows upward in height and outward in breadth. Where people are concerned, it is vitally important that growth is not confined to one or two particular areas of life but involves the whole person. Maturity has to do with wholeness. There is a beautiful description of the growth of the Lord Jesus in Luke 2:52, 'He grew in *wisdom* and *stature*, and in *favour with God* and *men*.' This is the kind of maturity you must seek to build into those in your house-group. Some people may have a very sound knowledge of the Scriptures but their home life may be a real mess. The answer is not to despise the growth that has taken place in one area, but to bring teaching and exhortation to show them that growth must also affect their relationship within their home.

Maturity means growing 'into Christ'. In Acts 11:25–26 we see how Paul and Barnabas spent a whole year teaching the church at Antioch. So effective was their ministry of building people up that these disciples were called 'Christians', adherents of Christ. They became 'little Christs'. The New Testament shows this to be the goal for each individual believer—to be 'conformed to the likeness of his Son, that he might be the firstborn among many brothers' (Rom 8:29). But there is also a corporate aspect to it. We don't come to this fulness on our own! Ephesians 4:11–16 describes how 'the body...grows and builds itself up in love, *as each part does its work.*' There is a corporateness to our growth. Our aim as the body of Christ is to become 'mature, attaining to the whole measure of the fulness of Christ' (v. 13). God's people growing up 'into the whole measure of the fulness of Christ' includes *character* (love, joy, peace, etc.), *power* (ability to do works of righteousness—including healing, prophecy, etc.), and *authority* (able to teach, rule, govern, overcome powers of darkness, etc.).

So our aim is to assist in that leadership ministry of bringing people to full maturity in Christ. The next chapters will deal with how to go about this. But it would be good to end this chapter by realizing the glorious truth that it doesn't all depend on you! *God* is at work in his people. The following scriptures should be constantly in your heart: Romans 8:28–29; Philippians 2:12–13; 2 Peter 1:3–4. There will be times when you may be almost overwhelmed by the problems that people have, and certainly your enemy, Satan, will not be slow to feed you with discouragement. But the truth is that God has determined to bring his people to maturity.

5

Teaching in the house group

Teaching is very important in the house group. What do we mean by 'teaching'? We can define it as 'the meaningful transmission of truth'. The mental image which many people have of 'teaching' in the church is that of the preacher standing up in the pulpit for forty-five minutes ('more' or 'less' according to your church background!), expounding the Scriptures to the congregation seated below. It can be a thrilling, interesting or boring experience depending upon the preacher and his theme, or a mixture of all three. But such a mental image cannot convey what must go on in your front room, neither does it describe the kind of relationship you are to have with those in your group. The Scriptures clearly show how important a place in his ministry Jesus gave to teaching, and how he used the situations, scenery and events in his life as vehicles for his teaching. You can see examples of this in Mark 9:33–37, Luke 10:38–42 and Mark 11:20–25. His teaching was life-orientated rather than formal, and your teaching in the house group must be similar if people's needs are to be met.

Knowing and doing

Right through the Bible we see tremendous emphasis on the importance of teaching. If you get a concordance and look at the first references to teaching you will find that the word is first used in Exodus 4:12 and 15, where God says he will teach Moses what to say (v. 12) and what to do (v. 15). Of course, that is not the first time teaching happened; Adam and Eve received teaching from God on the first day of their creation. But it is interesting to note that in those verses in Exodus we have the beginning of a thread which runs right through the Bible; that is, that teaching has a double purpose—namely, that we should *know* and *do*. This is brought out very strongly in Deuteronomy 32:47 where Moses said of God's commands and teaching, 'They are not just idle words for you—*they are your life'*.

The early church saw the importance of teaching. Acts 2:42 tells us how the new believers occupied themselves and in Acts 20:20 we see how Paul spent his time in Asia. Colossians 1:28 shows us how Christians come to maturity. There are scores of such passages in the Scriptures, all emphasizing this two-fold aspect of teaching—'knowing and doing'. Being sound in doctrine has nothing to do with having a 'certificate of orthodoxy' from an evangelical institution, but is much more related to knowing God and living worthily of him. In Titus 2:1 Paul tells Titus to teach the people what is in accord with sound doctrine. He then specifies what must be taught to various groups; to the older men, the older women, the younger men, the younger women, those who were slaves, and finally everybody (v. 11). Look carefully at this chapter and the 'sound doctrine' described in it, for it is just as vital for your house group today as it was for the Christians in Crete in A.D. 65!

One good teaching session each month

Having seen the importance of teaching, you will want to make it a regular part of your house-group life. It is a good idea to aim to have one good teaching session per month. For the purpose of this book we are assuming that the people in your house group will have been taught some basic doctrine when they came into your church. In our own church new converts and others wanting to join us are asked to go through an eight-week commitment course called 'How to join the church'. The course deals with repentance, faith, baptism in water, baptism in the Holy Spirit, life and relationships in the church, etc. The course runs concurrently with the evening service on Sundays and is taken by a different elder and his wife each week. After studying the week's subject there is opportunity for questions to be answered and prayer together before the group joins the rest of the church for coffee at the end of the service. Thus by the time they have finished the course each person should be grounded in basic truth as well as baptized in water and in the Holy Spirit. If the members of your house group have not received this basic teaching, you may find it necessary to teach some doctrine in the group, or at least to encourage people to study basic truth for themselves. Two good books to recommend are *Living God's Way* by Arthur Wallis and *Know the Truth* by Bruce Milne; or the course *How to join the Church,* by Richard Haydon-Knowell. But it is important that the people in your house group have a foundation of basic truth, so that they are able to understand the teaching they will receive in the house group and be able to relate it to the rest of the Scriptures.

To be a teacher you must also be a learner

If you are to teach others and help them grow in God you must be feeding on truth yourself. This means, as well as hearing truth preached on Sundays, you must be studying the Bible for yourself and growing in your understanding of God's word, ways and purposes. The Bible is a record of God's purposes for his people. The Old Testament describes his dealings with Israel, and this record is a 'model' for his ultimate and eternal purpose which is to be worked out through his church. If you look at 1 Corinthians 10:11 and Romans 15:4, you will see how God uses the Old Testament scriptures to show what he was going to bring about in his New Covenant people, the church, of which you are a part.

When you come to study the Bible, it is helpful to have a concordance and a Bible dictionary. Two other helpful books are *Pocket Guide to the Old Testament* by Cyril Bridgland and *Pocket Guide to the New Testament* by Francis Foulkes. Further Bible commentaries can be acquired according to your needs and pocket! There are several methods of Bible study, and it is good to vary the methods you use. Sometimes you will want to study one book, reading it right through several times and studying the background so that you can see where it fits into God's programme. You will 'soak up' the atmosphere of the book and understand the emotions and feeling of the writer; you will enter into the heartache of Isaiah and into the tears and joys of Paul the apostle. Let the experiences of these men speak to your own heart. Another method of study is to look at a theme of Scripture right through the Bible (e.g. salvation). Yet another is to study the life of a character such as Ezekiel or Peter and to learn from it.

Keep a notebook by you as you read, and write down the things that the Holy Spirit shows you from the Scriptures. There will be times when God will give you real personal direction from his word; when he does, obey him. Read Acts 16:6–12 and see how Paul's sensitivity and obedience to the prompting of the Holy Spirit meant that he was in exactly the right spot to get on a boat when God called him through a vision to go to Macedonia to preach the gospel.

Let God renew your mind as you read the Scriptures. Let him give you *his* perspective as you read about his dealings with his people and his present desires for them. Respond to God in prayer as you read ('Lord, your timing was perfect in that situation!') and make your Bible-reading a time of fellowship with him as well as a time of instruction and learning his ways.

Ways of teaching

There are several ways in which teaching is communicated to your house group, and all of them should figure in your leadership.

By example

A great deal of Jesus' teaching to the disciples was by example. It is, after all, one of the principal ways we learn! The best modern equivalent of this is the apprenticeship of a young trainee to a skilled craftsman. Look at John 13:12–15, where Jesus explains why he had washed his disciples' feet. Can you think of other instances where Jesus adopted this method of teaching? Paul sent young Timothy to the church at Ephesus and then writes to him and tells him to be an example of godly living (1 Tim 4:12).

We all need an example and pattern to follow. One of the tragedies in modern society is that most people today have grown up with scarcely any godly patterns upon which they can base their lives. All too often they repeat the failures of their parents' unhappy or broken relationships, ideals and ambitions. There is an urgent need today for a restoration of godly examples; the young people of our churches need this especially. As we said in an earlier chapter, your house group will learn as much from how you and your wife live as from what you say.

By instruction

Of course, example is not sufficient on its own. It must be accompanied by clear teaching of the word of God. In Romans 6:17 there is a remarkable picture of the way in which every child of God should be re-shaped by the truth. At one time we were slaves of sin—moulded, shaped and formed by the power of sin. But now, says the apostle, you Roman Christians have 'wholeheartedly obeyed the form of truth to which you were entrusted'. He had given to them a 'form of truth'—a structure of life-shaping and life-giving truth—and it had stamped its own image on them. Paul knew that the only way they could ever bear the image of Christ would be by receiving the whole doctrine and teaching of Christ, and as they obeyed it from the heart they would be shaped by it. Part of your task as a house-group leader will be, under the direction of the elders, to help provide that 'form of truth'. We will look more fully at what this entails in the section on 'How to teach'.

By admonition

The word 'admonition' can cause an immediate reaction. However, let us look at this very important word and see its real value. It means literally a 'putting in mind' from the Greek word *nouthesia* (*nous* = mind, *tithemi* = to put). It is to bring to a person's mind some truth—a word of encouragement, warning or rebuke. It is a 'face-to-face' word; not some general word to the mass hoping that somehow it will reach the intended target of Janet Sharp, but a word spoken to her directly, dealing with her specific need. It means saying to her *in private* (never in front of the group), 'Janet, I notice how often you get agitated that some people in the group seem so slow to learn—sometimes that comes across quite critically and hurtfully. You probably don't mean it to hurt, but I think Ephesians 4:29 shows a better way of achieving the same goal...' etc.

Take a look at Romans 15:14 (instruct = admonish); 1 Corinthians 4:14 (warn = admonish); Colossians 1:28 and 3:16 and note the context of this word 'admonish'. Admonishing does not mean to shame, expose, embarrass or tick off a person; it is to put a person 'in mind of' the truth in order to encourage him, to help him face up to a real need or problem. The goal is always the spiritual maturity of the believer, not the release of your pent-up frustration! Paul commands Timothy to 'correct, rebuke and encourage—with *great patience* and careful instruction' (2 Tim 4:2).

It is never easy to bring this word of admonition, but from time to time it is a necessary part of your wise and loving care of your group. It is another example of that earlier definition of teaching as the meaningful transmission of truth. It is important, too, that you are open to receive such admonition yourself from those who are over you in God if this should be necessary. Discipline and pruning are vital for all of us if we are to grow to maturity and live fruitful lives.

By prayer

You will learn quickly that however able a teacher you may be it is not enough. Paul was the great teacher in the church, yet having taught the Ephesian believers about the 'hope to which they had been called' and 'the glorious inheritance' and 'the great power available to us', he did not sit back and congratulate himself! Ephesians 1:17–18 shows us Paul praying his teaching through to the believers. Again and again you will find that you will need to pray the truth home as much as you teach it.

How to teach

There are three sources of teaching for your house group— the Sunday ministry heard each week in church, your own teaching material and other people's teaching material. We shall look at these in detail.

Applying the Sunday ministry

This will be one of the main ways of bringing teaching to the group. If the church is starting house groups for the first time, it would be particularly valuable if the pastor or elders could preach a short series to coincide with the starting of the groups. But whether the groups are new or not, what follows in this chapter will apply.

Make notes as you listen to the teaching on Sundays. Get your wife to do the same; you will get a fuller picture that way. In the days prior to the group meeting be asking God to show you the key things to share with the group. Talk and pray with your wife about it—learn to function as a team together. Decide whether you will let it lead into a discussion. If so, give some care and thought to preparing questions; if you are going to have discussion you will need to have at least three questions ready.

There are good and bad questions. You should aim to pose questions which draw out discussion rather than ones which merely require 'yes' or 'no' answers. For example, the question: 'What particular difficulties do you encounter when you pray?' is more likely to provoke open and useful discussion than the question: 'Has anyone anything to say about this passage?'

At the beginning of house group, announce that you will be leading a discussion on the Sunday ministry. At the appropriate time, give a brief résumé (maximum 5 minutes) of the sermon or teaching session. State the particular points upon which you want to focus (the idea is *not* to have a 're-hash' of last Sunday's food!) and then lead in with your first question. It is a good idea to put it to someone in the group whom you know will be able to 'start the ball rolling'.

Draw other people in, and be aware of those who are new Christians. You may have to interject, 'Bob, when John spoke about the tabernacle being a 'type' of the church, what he meant was....' Don't let the discussion become a free-for-all. Bear in mind that you are aiming to teach the group those two or three specific things you asked God about. Make sure that you return to them again and again. Summarize at the end and then turn it into action and application. For example, 'Let's ask God to write that truth on our hearts in prayer right now', or 'This is going to mean that we begin to have a different attitude about....' Don't forget, teaching is the *meaningful* transmission of truth!

Preparing your own teaching material

Earlier in the chapter we recommended keeping a note-book as you study your Bible, so that you have a record of things you have learned from God. Ask God to make you

like the man in Matthew 13:52 who had a house with a
well-stocked storeroom. Your notebook will soon become
such a 'storeroom' from which you will have 'treasures' to
bring out for your house group.

There are three aspects which are important when you
come to prepare teaching for the house group. They are
'preparation', 'presentation' and 'application'.

Preparation. Prepare thoroughly. Don't just hope it will
'be all right on the night'! Know what you want to say. Put it
down in an easy-to-read form. Underline your main points.

Presentation. Don't be too long. Fifteen minutes should
be long enough to lead in with the teaching. Try and give a
clear framework to what you are going to say. Here is an
example:

'Tonight we are going to look at Romans 5:1–5. Let's
break the passage down into the following sections:

1. What it means to be justified by faith.
2. The results of justification
    a) peace with God
    b) access into grace
    c) rejoicing in hope of glory of God
    d) rejoicing in suffering.
3. Why it's possible to rejoice in suffering
    a) because we know suffering does something
    b) because God's love is poured into our hearts.

Application. (Continuing to use this passage of Scripture
as an example.) There is obviously a lot that could be said
about such a wonderful passage, but all you will need to do
is to open it up in the way we have described. Then lead a
time of sharing, perhaps by asking the following questions
(allowing 15 minutes or so for each).

1. Why is it so important to know that you have peace with
    God, and can that peace be affected in any way?
2. Have you had any experiences which confirm that
    suffering produces perseverance, character and hope?
3. (If time) How would you describe this experience of
    verse 5?

There will be times when a discussion is not the best way of applying the teaching. If you have been speaking about prayer, worship, relationships or perhaps the gift of prophecy, it may be better to lead the group in a time of prayer, praise or breaking bread (communion). It is important that you apply the teaching so that people have an opportunity (either at the meeting or later) of being 'doers' of the word as well as 'hearers'. Understanding is not enough. Teaching must always lead to action—that is how people come to maturity.

Using other teaching material

It can sometimes be helpful to use an article in a Christian magazine or something similar as the basis for your teaching. Let everyone know well in advance so that they can obtain copies. Ask all the members of the group to be prepared to share what has helped them from this article.

Books such as *Knowing God* by J. Packer lend themselves to this type of group study. The Coastlands teaching manuals (we have already mentioned *How to Join the Church*) are particularly geared for group study. They include *How to be a Worshipper*, *How to Study the Bible* and *How to be sure of the Bible*.

When you or your wife read a book which is particularly helpful you can recommend it to the people in your group. If you do not have a great deal of time for reading, there may be a reliable person in your group who is not only a voracious reader but sound in doctrine and who will be glad to read books for you and let you know which ones will be helpful for people in your group. Your pastor or elders will be able to recommend helpful doctrinal books. Your wife will find it useful to have a list of books which are particularly helpful for women. If she is not a wide reader, it would be a good idea for her to ask for such a list from someone who has already compiled one.

Another study method for people in the group

You can encourage folk in your group to study during the week by introducing 'Buddy System Bible Study'. Quite a number of the women in our own church find this a helpful way to study and it is easy to organize for women who are at home during the day. Two married couples could also use this method; or two Christians working the same hours at the same place, during their lunch-break. Two friends (or 'buddies'!) arrange to meet weekly to go through a section of the Bible—for instance, the epistle to the Philippians. They are given a sheet of paper on which is written a short outline of the epistle with background information, followed by sections marked 'Week 1', 'Week 2', etc. The whole epistle takes eight weeks. Each section starts with the passage to be read by each 'buddy' during the week, followed by two questions to be discussed at the weekly study together. The first two weeks' sections might look like this:

Week 1: Philippians 1:1–11

1. What does Paul pray for these believers?
2. Go through the passage and discover all that it says about Paul's relationship with the Christians at Philippi. How did he feel about them?

Week 2: Philippians 1:12–26

1. How has Paul's imprisonment led to the advance of the gospel?
2. What does Paul mean when he says 'to me, to live is Christ'? What does this statement mean in your life?

If there are people in your group who want to do this you will need to find or prepare the studies for them; or possibly your pastor or elders would do this for you, particularly if a number of house groups are asking for it. Studies can be photocopied or duplicated so that they are available to everyone. It is necessary to prepare several studies initially, as some pairs of 'buddies' will race through their first sheet quickly and be ready for another, while other pairs will move at a slower pace. This is a helpful way of studying the Bible, and the 'buddies' can be changed over every so often so that different people get to know one another as they study together.

Watch for potential teachers

Look out for members of your house group who may be developing the ability to teach. When you find someone who has that potential, give him the opportunity occasionally to take a teaching session with the group. Discuss with him afterwards the way he led the session, encouraging him where he did well and talking with him about ways in which he could improve. It will help you as the leader to have another person upon whom you can call for this kind of support, and it will help the group member to realize his potential as someone to whom God has given the ability to teach.

6

Sharing and caring in the house group

The church is a family, and families share (or should do!).
There is a real need for Christians to be open with one
another in the family of God. Within the larger congregational gathering it is almost impossible to share with one
another the joys, blessings and difficulties which we experience. However, within the smaller unit of the house
group this kind of mutual care, encouragement and support
can begin to take place. As the individuals in the group
begin to grow together in relationship there will come a
desire to share what is happening in their lives with the
others in the group when they meet together. Wisdom is
needed as you lead the group in this; but where people
share with sensitivity there will come a richness and reality
in relationships with one another.

Sharing will lead to caring. As people get to know each
other better it will soon become apparent to them that
belonging to each other means caring for each other. We
are to 'carry each other's burdens, and in this way you will
fulfil the law of Christ' (Gal 6:2). There should be no needy
or lonely people in God's family.

The basis for family life

This concept of 'family' is very important in the Scriptures
and therefore in the church. One of the key New Testament

words to describe this relationship among God's people is 'fellowship' (Greek = *koinonia*). The word means 'having a share with someone in something'. The way it is used in Luke 5:10 throws light on its meaning as it describes Peter's relationship with James and John. It is the same Greek word *koinonia*. The thing they had a share in together was the fishing business. That's why they went to each other's aid when they were in trouble and why they pooled their catches.

Now let us see what the basis is for this fellowship or partnership among God's people. From Galatians 3:26–28 it is clear that the only basis for fellowship is that all believers are *in Christ*. Our fellowship is not based on being Jews or Greeks, slaves or free, male or female, or anything else. The primary ground of our fellowship is that we have a share in Christ together. It is this which makes the church different from a Christian Union or any other Christian organization where the primary basis is the fact that all the members are nurses or students or pilots or postmen—albeit Christians.

It is vital that you understand that the basis for house-group fellowship is the same as the basis for church fellowship—your being 'in Christ together'. That is the only distinctive characteristic you should foster; not that you are a group of 'intellectuals' or 'discussers' or that the group is built around your own ministry or personality, but simply that you are 'in Christ'. Anything else will have in it the seeds of division and will prevent people coming to full maturity. If the primary basis is that you are all good discussers, musicians, pray-ers, etc., people will be 'overgrown' in that direction, and others who are not 'good discussers' etc. will feel left out. Paul sets the ideal for us in Ephesians 4:15–16 and these two verses deserve careful study.

Being members one of another

We see, then, that the basis for our family life is that we are all 'in Christ'. We are all part of his body (1 Cor 12:12–27) and we all have an important part to play in the life of the body. We *need* one another! Our involvement, acceptance and care of one another is inherent in our belonging. The following scriptures will show you the kind of behaviour which expresses our identification with one another: Romans 12:10; 13:8; 15:7,14; 16:16; Galatians 5:13, Ephesians 4:2, 29–32; 5:21. (There are, of course, many other scripture passages which speak of the way Christians should behave toward each other. But if we just did these particular things, what a difference it would make!)

Your role as leader

You and your wife have a very important role in this development of the family life of your group; relationships will develop and mature under wise and stable leadership. Let us consider 1 Thessalonians 2:7–8 and 11–12. Paul speaks of himself and those who were ministering with him as being like a mother (gentle and caring) and a father (encouraging, comforting and urging). The word 'mother' here means 'a nurse', and the thought behind this is that these were not children handed over to a hired nurse but that Paul *himself* was a 'mother-nurse' to them. Paul is saying here that the roles of mother and of father were combined in the same person(s). This is what leadership should mean to you and your wife; you are to be mother/father to your house group. All of these gentle and firm attributes will be required.

Being a mother is demanding (as you may know!). Children are not with you just from 9 a.m. until 5 p.m. They are a twenty-four hour commitment and do not have their problems, needs and demands at your convenience. In a family there are things happening all the time, and a mother's greatest contribution is to be *available*—as a shoulder to weep on, an example to follow, a healer of hurts, a solver of problems, a sharer of joys, etc. A father needs to be an encourager (1 Thess 2:11). This is the same word that the Lord Jesus gives to the Holy Spirit—the Paraclete or encourager. It literally means 'to call to one's side' (*para* = beside, *kaleo* = to call). Paul came alongside in response to their need. Again we see that relationships are vitally important. You will need to 'come alongside' people and to encourage an attitude within the group where no one 'walks by on the other side'. The way you and your wife 'mother' and 'father' the group will establish a pattern. The way you share yourselves with them will help them to do the same with each other. We have noticed how often people reproduce the attitudes and actions of their leaders.

One of our newer couples in house-group leadership told us, 'When we were in our old house group Len, our leader, was a man who really prayed. He prayed with us as a group, so we were a group that learnt to pray—but he also prayed with us as individuals if we had a need or a problem. Len would see it through, too; it wasn't just a case of praying then forgetting it. He would make a note of the problem then keep on praying about it and be in touch frequently to see if prayer had been answered! So when we became group leaders we decided to do the same—to make our group a praying group, one that would keep going until God answered.'

Take the lead in sharing

In the house-group meeting itself, your example will largely determine the response of your group members in the matter of sharing openly. It is easy to share joyful, positive news and information; but if you hold back from sharing a personal or family need (for example, the possibility of redundancy in your job or the fact that your child is having difficulties at school), you should not be surprised if your group members are equally reticent and reluctant to share.

If you are aware that you have a tendency to hold back from sharing, ask yourself why. Do you feel vaguely ashamed at the possibility of being made redundant and that people may regard you as a failure in some way? Or are you deeply threatened by the possibility of being unable to provide for your family adequately? Do you feel unhappy about communicating your child's school problem, fearing that people will criticize you as a parent? Be honest and search your heart for the real reasons behind your reluctance to share. If you find that pride (or fear) is the cause you will need to face up to this, confess it before God, turn from it and see that your real security lies in him, not in the maintaining of a 'good' reputation. Only then will you be free and able to walk openly with your brothers and sisters in the group and receive their love and caring concern which you and your wife need as much as every other person in the group.

You will find that as you are prepared to share your needs, the rest of your group will be encouraged to do so as well. (There will obviously be some needs and problems, perhaps relating to people in the group, which you will *not* share with the group but with your elders or minister; we are referring in this chapter to the needs 'common to man' which affect us all at various times and which can be shared and talked about within the group context.) It is important to remind your group about the need for confidentiality. If someone shares a need or a burden it should be contained within the group; unless, of course, the person makes it very clear that he is happy for it to be mentioned further afield.

Occasionally someone may begin to share a problem which you realize would be better shared in private. The best way of dealing with this is to break in gently, 'Bob, I feel that it would be best if you and I could chat about this together rather than share it in the group right now. Are you free to pop round tomorrow evening? We can talk about it then.' The chapter 'Counselling individuals in the house group' may be helpful to you in following up this kind of situation.

Praying for one another

A time of sharing needs will usually be followed by a time of intercessory prayer and waiting on God. (More about this in the chapter on 'Praying in the house group'). As leader you will need to encourage others to take part. As the people in the group grow in their relationship together this will happen much more readily; their understanding and recognition of one another's needs will help them to participate in prayer and in other ways. Also, as people become confident in and aware of the acceptance and love of others in the group they will begin to lose their shyness and respond to your encouragement to take part actively in the group meeting.

Socializing is important

Socializing is important in the house group. There may be some traditionally-minded folk who feel quite happy in a Bible study but slightly uncomfortable if house-group night takes the form of a ramble or a Monopoly evening! These people need to be helped to understand the function of a house group (see chapter 1). We need to learn to relax together and to relate on all kinds of levels, otherwise genuine friendships cannot easily develop or grow. You need to plan opportunities for people to meet together. On some house-group evenings it is a good idea to split the group into units of three or four people meeting in different homes for a meal together; this gives people an opportunity to get to know one another in a smaller group. There are many other possibilities. The group can plan a weekend at a conference centre, a Saturday outing, a meal together, a swim night, a games evening, etc. These activities should be occasional rather than regular, and of course if a weekend away is planned for the whole house group the elders would find it helpful to know in advance. But we need to remember that we are family and that we are whole people; this means that our life together must include more than just studying the Bible and praying. Experience has shown that times of relaxing together greatly enhance our fellowship at other levels.

Breaking bread together

Breaking bread occasionally in a communion meal will help to unite the group together in the Lord's presence in a beautiful way. It is interesting that the context of this special remembrance of Christ's victorious and triumphant death is an ordinary meal (*see* Luke 22:14, Acts 2:46 and 1 Corinthians 11:20–34). As one New Testament scholar put it, 'A congregation which does not eat hot dogs in real fellowship is not able to celebrate the Lord's supper in the right way'. Within the house group both sorts of eating need to be done, and it is important to understand the benefits of each.

Sharing with unbelievers

There will be times when you want to use the house group evangelistically, and to plan an evening when friends who are not Christians can be invited to an informal meal followed by testimonies and a film or a presentation of the gospel in some definite way. In our own fellowship we have sometimes planned these to be linked with Christmas or some other celebration—and in summer they can take the form of a barbecue evening or a garden picnic.

We have already seen that house groups are for the building up and strengthening of Christians in order that they may grow to maturity. For this to happen there must be real commitment and openness to one another as brothers and sisters in the Lord. It is not possible for this to take place if the group is always being visited by non-Christians, even though they may be folk who are interested in hearing the gospel or asking questions about the Christian faith. Yet there is real value in using the house group for evangelism on a fairly regular basis. Part of the 'bringing to maturity' of God's people is in teaching them to reproduce; and regular, well-planned evangelistic evenings in which the whole group is involved in praying, planning, inviting people and sharing testimonies can be very effective and may well reach people who are not open to the idea of 'coming to church'. Visitors to the house-group evening who show genuine interest in knowing more will obviously be invited to church on a Sunday, and those who come to real faith in Jesus will then be brought into a commitment group and ultimately linked into a house group by the elders.

It is not wise to evangelize from the house group until it has become a united, loving, caring and praying entity. When this is a reality, the love that exists between the members will be an important part of the group's witness.

Serving one another

Sharing and caring will mean 'serving' one another with glad and willing hearts. Every person in every house group has a gift or a talent and you, as the leader, will need to be aware of those individual talents and of your responsibility to encourage every person in your group to use that special ability for the benefit of others (1 Pet 4:10). Some people may feel that they do not have any talents or abilities; you will need to help them to see that they do, and that their talent is valuable to the others in the group. Some may be very shy and unwilling to reveal their gifts; you will need to help them be more outgoing.

There are many ways you can help people develop and share their talents. Sometimes you can recommend a book for them to read. For instance, if a person wants to increase in the gift of hospitality, or begin entertaining people for the first time, a book like *The Pleasure of Your Company* by Dale Garratt might be helpful. A 'Crafts and Hobbies' evening one week will give people an opportunity to display their expertise at making things and to share their interests and knowledge. Those whose particular interest is cookery can supply some special refreshments for the evening. Folk who are particularly good at DIY and decorating can give help to someone else in the group who is not able to tackle this; and non-gardeners would no doubt welcome help and advice from those who enjoy getting to grips with plants and weeds. You, as leader of the group, should know who has needs, and who has gifts and abilities to meet those needs; and you will find real joy in encouraging your group members to serve one another.

This can also apply in the wider context of the church; as you liaise with other house-group leaders you will find that among the house groups there is an amazing diversity of talent which can be brought into action where it is needed. This will extend from things like painting and decorating right through to drama and mime. Consider the possibility of your church putting on an original gospel presentation which would involve not only the writers, singers, actors and musicians but also the painters and decorators (scenery), the needlework experts (costumes), the craft workers (props) and the cooks (refreshments at the end!).

God-given talents need to be used, and will bless those who give and those who receive. You need to make opportunity for this in the house group and beyond. Don't forget that there will be those whose talents and gifts lie in the areas of friendship, encouragement of others, listening and counselling. These folk can be of real help to you in your ministry—use them.

Caring for one another

You and your wife will have realized by now that *by yourselves* you could not possibly provide total care or meet all the needs of your house group. You were never meant to! The idea is not for you to do it all, but to motivate each to care for one another under your guidance. Let us look at some specific ways of putting this into action on a personal level. We will identify some of the immediate needs in your group and then see how (or rather *through whom*) they can best be met.

Immediate needs

a) Pam Sore obviously needs help. She has four children who, like herself and Paul, have suffered the trauma of marriage break-up, and the sudden increase of her family from three to six has made organization of house-work, budgeting, etc., very difficult.

b) Bill and Helen, you remember, are poised between going on in God and lapsing back into traditionalism.

c) Robert Old just needs loving and some practical help around the house. Being on his own after having had a loving wife for forty-three years comes very hard— especially at weekends. Sunday lunch for one isn't much fun!

d) Janet Sharp feels the same about Sundays!

e) Bob New still doesn't know who Deuteronomy is!

f) Jill and Heather miss home very much and long to have someone to drop in on when the pressures of their worldly art college threaten to overwhelm them.

How these needs could be met

a) Pam's needs can only really be met by another mum. You and your wife could very well ask Pat to make a point of helping Pam; perhaps by spending a morning with her on a regular basis—not just to have coffee and a chat but to actually help her with some of her specific problems. Pat will need to approach it wisely, but if they both understand that they belong to each other and that they are to serve and love one another it should be possible to work out the kind of practical help that Pam needs.

b) Bill and Helen's needs can't be met quite so obviously—

or can they? Do you think they could be just the couple for Jill and Heather to 'adopt' as a term-time Mum and Dad? They would be really good for each other; Bill and Helen could catch something of the girls' zeal and enthusiasm and they could give so much in return.

c) A discreet word to some of the couples to invite Robert Old for a Sunday on a fairly regular basis would be the answer. Janet could come as well. What about suggesting, too, that they occasionally do some entertaining themselves? All too often single people neglect this, yet there is no reason at all why they should not entertain.

d) John has begun to feel a sense of responsibility regarding Bob New. Probably the answer is to put this on a proper footing. You should ask John to see Bob once a week and take him through some basic teaching. He can start by telling him about Deuteronomy!

Obviously these are very apparent needs, and most of them are long-term, but every house group is going to have such situations. Pray together with your wife about the ways in which various needs can be met. Bear in mind what we mentioned earlier, that it need not always be through your own house-group members. You may have an A-level maths student in your group who badly needs some extra coaching; another house group may have a maths teacher who is happy to help.

Other practical needs may be connected with the house-group meeting itself. Someone may need transport to the meeting each week if it is too far to walk; this will mean arranging for someone in the group who has a car to call for them on the way and take them home afterwards. For some couples finding a baby-sitter can be a problem. In our own church, half of the house groups meet on Wednesday evening and the other half on Thursday evening; this enables 'Thursday night-ers' to baby-sit for couples on Wednesday nights and vice versa. If it is not possible for a couple to find a regular weekly baby-sitter, they may need your help in organizing a rota of people who will sit for them once a month so that all the house-group meetings are covered.

In our church we have encouraged house-group leaders to appoint an 'administrator' who will not only liaise with the Church Administrator or Secretary, but will also look after matters like arrangements for transport, outings and other practical details concerning the house group. This has proved to be greatly beneficial and gives a real opportunity for someone (male or female) to serve the group.

Financial needs

Fellowship involves finance. The Bible has a great deal to say about this; you can see from Acts 2:45 and Acts 4:34–35 that it was one of the beautiful marks of the early church. The apostle Paul has important things to say about the matter of sharing our substance with those in need (see Romans 12:13, 1 Timothy 6:18 and Hebrews 13:16).

In practice, as far as your house group is concerned, it will mean that John and Janet (who both earn good salaries) will not only tithe into the general needs of the church but will also help Jill and Heather with the cost of the church camping holiday they would otherwise be unable to afford. Bill and Helen might possibly give another young couple some help with their high mortgage payments as their own house was paid for several years ago. In our own church, one girl was refused a grant for a final additional year of her college course. Her house group committed themselves to supporting her financially through that year, which they faithfully did.

We must make sure that we act responsibly where finance is concerned, and we would stress here that we are talking about financial sharing between people who are *committed* to one another and known to one another and to the elders of the church. Too often in the past 'the church' has been known as the place to go for a 'soft touch' or a 'quick hand-out' to anyone with a hard-luck story, while at the same time having a reputation for 'always asking for money'.

The New Testament has clear directions for God's people about the use of money—and the kind of financial commitments we have just mentioned, though they may sound revolutionary to us, were normal New Testament practice!

7

Worshipping in the house group

It's Wednesday night, and the house group pours into your home. It feels good to be together again; you look around at the warm glowing faces of Heather and Jill as they animatedly discuss how a friend at college is beginning to take an interest in the Christian faith. John and Bob are talking about a book John has just finished reading. Others are chatting together. You glance at the clock—twenty past eight. You give a cough.

'I think we'll start tonight with a time of worship,' you announce. 'I'd like to teach you a new song. I'm not too sure of the tune, but perhaps you can try and pick it up on the guitar, John.' Ten minutes later, after a rather embarrassed group have endeavoured to follow your slightly off-key singing, you say, 'Oh, well, the words are good, anyway! Perhaps we should sing something different—who's got a song we all know?' Pat calls out, 'Let's have "In the name of Jesus we have the victory". It was such a blessing when we sang it last week.' You sing it, but somehow the anointing isn't there as you struggle through it tonight.

You are beginning to feel that it's one of those evenings. Maybe, you think to yourself, prayer will be the answer. 'Let's pray together, and tell God what's really on our hearts,' you say. After a longish pause Robert Old begins to pray one of his deep theological prayers praising God for his sovereignty and providential care of God's people down through the ages. Funny—somehow it doesn't seem to have brought the sense of heaven into our hearts! At last he's stopped. Oh, now Pam is praying, 'Lord, what's on my heart is how I've failed you today—shouting at the kids and then Paul when he came home. I'm sorry, Lord.' Well, at least she's being real; but somehow it isn't exactly worship. Oh dear, now Janet will probably pray one of her prayers to try and get things back on course. Yes—she's starting....'

In describing this imaginary situation some things have obviously been exaggerated, but such a 'time of worship' could conceivably happen. Look back over the situation. What went wrong, and why? Basically, it went wrong because of a lack of understanding on the part of the leader and the group about the nature of worship and the priesthood of the people of God. 1 Peter 2:5 says this: 'You also, like living stones, are being built into a spiritual house to be a holy priesthood, offering spiritual sacrifices acceptable to God through Jesus Christ.' This verse speaks about a house becoming a priesthood. In the Old Testament the priesthood worshipped *in* a house, but now the believers *are* that house. They are being built together to become a priesthood to God in order to offer up praise and worship. As the house-group leader you will need to lead the people in your group into that praise and worship.

What is worship?

A. W. Tozer defines worship as 'a feeling deep within our hearts of awe, love for, delight and humble admiration of God'. There is something about God that causes a response deep within our hearts—we *feel* something! We feel gratitude, appreciation and love for the mighty God who has cleansed us from sin through the blood of his Son and brought us into his family. We feel a strong desire to give him glory, praise and adoration; worship is the expression of that.

How are we to worship?

What should be the prime characteristic of Christian worship? Philippians 3:3 says that true worship is 'by the Spirit'—it proceeds from a people whose whole personalities are renewed and energized by the Holy Spirit.

(It follows, therefore, that the members of your house group must be people who have a clear experience of the baptism in the Spirit. Without this they will not be able to really enter into worship 'by the Spirit'. If there are any in your group who have not yet received this, make it a priority to see that they are led into it as soon as possible.)

Graham Kendrick, in his book *Worship* (recommended for everyone who wants to know more about worship and especially leading worship), says that this kind of worship is

> to tap into the very source of worship himself, the inexhaustible, endlessly praising Spirit of God, and to allow him liberty to join with our own spirit in expressing through our mind and body the worth of our saviour Jesus, and the love of our heavenly Father. (Page 91.)

As the group leader you must learn to lead your people into worship where there is a real openness to and dependence upon the Holy Spirit; a freedom to respond to his leading and a real sense of being a holy priesthood to God. If you are to do this, you must be a real worshipper yourself, able to stir up your own spirit to glorify and praise God.

Worship in the group

It is a good idea to set aside part of the evening (not necessarily every week) for praise and worship. Before you start remind the group that you are coming to worship a God who is infinitely worthy of their praise. Some (including you!) may have had a hard day and not feel motivated to worship, so it is good to focus on the fact that God is worthy and that he desires our praise even if it is a matter of will rather than desire for some. It would be good to remind them of the words of Habakkuk 3:16–18, where he determined to rejoice in God in spite of the dreadful circumstances he was facing. Begin worship by reminding God's people of who they are, perhaps singing a song together which encourages them to recognize afresh that they are a priesthood to him. There are a number of songs which express this; for example, 'Come and praise him, royal priesthood', 'Within the veil I long to come' or 'Draw near to God and he'll draw near to you'. As you sing such a song, perhaps several times, the Holy Spirit will make these words alive in the hearts of the worshippers. Let that song then lead on to one of direct worship or praise to God (rather than just encouragement to worship). Songs such as 'You are the King of glory', 'I love you, Lord, and I lift my voice' or 'Who is like unto thee?' Make sure your musician knows the songs well and that you (or someone who is musical if you are not) can give a clear, confident lead. If you do not have a competent musician in the group, it is probably better to do without one; an incompetent musician is a distraction rather than a help. Instruct the group as to the purpose of singing. It is not a time for favourite choruses, nor of singing one song after another, but of using songs intelligently to express to God your love, appreciation and joy in him. Encourage people to sing in harmony in tongues as the Spirit enables them to, and to be open to gifts of the Spirit that will build each other up.

Teach as you go

Don't be afraid to teach people how to worship. You may need to say, later on in the proceedings, 'You remember while we were singing "You are the King of glory" there was such a sense of the presence of God with us. But then someone began singing "Bind us together". What happened was that one moment we were worshipping and caught up with the Lord, and the next we were thinking about each other. That kind of sudden switch in direction generally interrupts the flow of worship. It's the same when we pray—if we are all praising God and suddenly someone starts praying for a ceasefire in the Middle East we'll be in confusion. We need to be sensitive to the leading and direction of the Spirit.' Such teaching needs to be loving and wise, for then it will help to build a people who really know how to worship by the Spirit.

People who cannot worship freely

There are some people who find difficulty in worshipping God freely. Some are self-conscious about praying aloud, raising their hands in praise, etc. If this is the case, it may help to sing a song such as 'Lord, make me an instrument of worship' and to suggest that everyone raises their hands as they sing the line 'I'll lift up my hands in your name'. Doing something with twelve other people makes it easier to do on your own another time.

As we said earlier, your own example as a worshipper will help. Some may not be able to worship freely because they are not yet baptized in the Spirit; here the answer is obvious. Some may be unable to worship because they are not living righteously or there is unconfessed sin or an unforgiving attitude in their lives; if after talking with them you find this to be the case, they need to be shown how seriously God regards this and encouraged to confess, repent and put things right. There are those who find it hard to worship because they are not reading the Scriptures or enjoying fellowship with God in prayer; worship springs from relationship, and if the relationship is not being cultivated the worship will not flow! Some may be shy simply because they have never worshipped freely before and it is all new to them.

As the weeks pass you will notice those who are having difficulties in worship and you can spend time with them and lovingly draw them out to find the source of the problem. If you feel out of your depth with a person's difficulties in worship, share this with your elders and seek their help. It may be good for your minister or one of your elders to visit the house group one week to speak about worship; tell your group that at the following week's house-group evening you will spend some time worshipping and putting into practice the things you have learned.

Use of spiritual gifts

Let's go back to the house group in the front room for a few minutes. This evening, in contrast to that rather disastrous time of worship described earlier, the group offered up to God praise and worship which was worthy of him. Afterwards they felt that their understanding and appreciation of God had grown and that somehow they had been spiritually built up and strengthened. Several things happened during the worship. John prayed in tongues and Janet brought the interpretation. It was full of praise to God for his wonderful wisdom in making them all one new man in Christ. At the end of the interpretation they all felt that God had revealed truth to them very powerfully by the Holy Spirit. Later on Brian spoke a word of prophecy; it spoke of God's delight in them and that his choosing of them had not been aimless or indiscriminate but full of purpose. That purpose was that they might reveal his glory on the earth. As the prophecy continued they had all felt that God was speaking directly to them and they had responded by resolving to obey in the matters about which he had spoken.

1 Corinthians 12, 13 and 14 are chapters which relate to the exercise of spiritual gifts in the church. At the beginning of chapter 12 Paul says, 'I do not want you to be ignorant about spiritual gifts', so you should make a point of carefully studying these chapters. On that particular house-group evening those gifts of tongues, interpretation and prophecy were, in the words of 1 Corinthians 12:7, a 'manifestation

of the Holy Spirit'. It was the Holy Spirit showing himself and doing things. He chose to reveal himself through John, Janet and Brian in those particular ways, enabling them to speak as they did. It was they who did the speaking, and in the case of Janet and Brian it was in English and in words familiar to them, but what they said was what the Spirit of God wanted to say. What was the purpose of these manifestations? 1 Corinthians 12:7 and 14:26 tell us that manifestations of the Spirit are given for 'the common good' and for the 'strengthening of the church'. John, Janet, Brian and some of the others in the group have been earnestly desiring the common good of all and the strengthening of God's people. This desire and openness to the Spirit is important (1 Corinthians 14:1) and it was because of this that the Spirit could use them.

Freedom and control

As a leader you will need to encourage people and provide a 'safe environment' for these gifts that Paul speaks about to be exercised. You will need to teach the following truths:

1. That the Spirit is willing to use 'each one' (12:7).
2. That we all need each other (12:21).
3. That mutual love is essential (chapter 13).
4. That tongues is usually prayer, praise, adoration and thanksgiving to God in languages given by the Spirit (14:2, 13–18), though at times God may choose to speak 'directly' to his people through the interpretation of a tongue.
5. That tongues need to be interpreted when used publicly (14:13).
6. That prophecy is God speaking to men and women and that it is to build up and not pull down God's people (14:3).
7. That women may pray and prophesy but they are not to do the public weighing of prophecy; that is the function of men with a clear prophetic gift. In this respect women

are to be silent (14:29–35). This is a possible explanation of the injunction in verse 34. Alternatively the silence which is commanded could be a prohibition against women engaging in 'dialogue' regarding the doctrine, as the men did in their more discursive manner of teaching. This would be in harmony with what Paul says in 2 Timothy 2:11. Some commentators regard this as an injunction against chattering, but according to W. E. Vine this meaning is absent from the use of the verb 'speak' (Greek *laleo*) everywhere else in the New Testament. It is to be understood in the same sense as in verses 2, 3–6, 4, 11, 13, 18, 19, 21, 23, 27–29 and 39.

8. That the other manifestations (or gifts) of the Spirit, such as those listed in chapter 12:7–11, are just as needful when the situation calls for them.

9. That prophecy needs to be weighed (14:29). This does not just mean asking 'Was it from God?', because it is obvious that anything contradicting Scripture would be immediately suspect; it also means asking very definitely, 'What is God saying to us?' or, 'Is there any action that we need to take?'

These general guidelines given by the apostle Paul are to encourage the use of spiritual gifts to ensure that the church is built up and strengthened. You will find that when people begin to exercise these gifts, your reassurance that what was said or done was right will be very important. Make a practice of speaking to people afterwards (perhaps over coffee) and chatting to them about it; if correction or direction is needed it should be done in the same way. Most people will be learners and will value your encouragement and counsel. If correction is needed you should not need to bring it during the meeting unless it is a very serious error and definitely harmful. If a person in the group frequently brings forth prophecy or visions about which you have doubts or reservations, you will need to share this with your elders for them to take some action. Generally, though, correction is very seldom required. You may sometimes need to encourage a person to speak out the interpretation of a tongue if he or she is hesitant to do so.

It is helpful to teach people not to expect that the Spirit will always say or do the same thing through them. Some people never experience any gift of the Spirit beyond speaking in tongues—but these chapters encourage us to be open to the Spirit being manifested through us in *many* different ways.

Encourage people to worship in private

If people are worshippers in private they will worship in the house group and in church. Learn to excel in worship yourself, and share with your group how to go about it. Don't just worship when you have your 'quiet time'; be in continual fellowship with the Lord through the day. Get into the habit of overflowing with thanksgiving (Col 1: 11–12; Eph 5:20) as you consider your right of access into God's presence (Rom 5:1–2). Consciously enjoy the love of God which has been poured into your heart through the Holy Spirit (Rom 5:5). Remember that the joy of the Lord is your strength, and that joy is released in you as you praise and thank God. Use the gift of tongues frequently; you don't have to speak out loud! Prayer in tongues can be flowing as you go about your work through the day, and it will edify you and build you up in your faith (1 Cor 14:4). Learn to be creative in your private worship of God, and encourage your group in this. You will find that it will carry over when you worship as a group, so that your worship will not only include praise and the use of spiritual gifts but also spontaneous songs of praise, relevant reading of Scripture, the sharing of a poem or song that God gave somebody yesterday, kneeling in silent adoration or dancing with joy before the Lord.

True worship will allow God to manifest himself among his people. Graham Kendrick expresses this graphically in the last chapter of his book.

> True worship is bound to reveal more of the character of Jesus, and he is described in Scripture as both a Lion and a Lamb. If our worship is to become real, then this is who will walk among us, at times in gentleness and at times in fearsome grandeur. I long, and at the same time rightly fear, to hear more of the mighty roar of the Lion of Judah in our worship, for there is a need in our times to regain first-hand knowledge of the awesome majesty and power of Jesus. Judah in fact means 'praise', so Jesus is literally the Lion of praise, as well as the sacrificial Lamb who was led meekly to the slaughter. Ultimately, the central issue in our decision to pursue true worship is whether or not we are willing for this Jesus to walk among us as our King. If we are indeed willing, then we have begun the journey. (Page 205.)

8

Praying in the house group

Prayer, as well as worship, is an important part of house-group life. It is exciting to see God visibly at work in answer to prayer; the members of your group will grow in faith as they see God move in one another's lives and in the church. You, as leader, must help to establish them in a prayer life that is real and vital. Does the thought of that thrill you or terrify you? Your answer will depend very much on the quality of your personal prayer life.

Your own prayer life

It is a fact that your personal prayer life will be reflected in the prayer life of your house group. If the members of your group know that you are committed to becoming a man of prayer, they will want to grow in that area also. If your prayer life is strong and joyful, they will aim for that, too. The opposite also applies—if you find prayer dry and boring, they will probably feel the same way. What you are speaks more loudly than what you say!

How do you use your prayer time?

Take a good look at the way you use your personal prayer time, and give real attention to what we said about worship in the previous chapter. Start your prayer time with worship; focusing upon God in all his power, love and glory will cause your faith to rise as you begin to pray about the various matters which concern you. As the leader of your group, you will be very aware of the needs and problems of those in your charge, and you will often be bringing them before the Lord in prayer and intercession. Remind yourself constantly that it is *God's* power which changes people, and your praying will release God's power in that person's life. A long-term counselling situation with someone in your group will be helped immeasurably by constant and believing prayer for the person concerned. As you pray, God will give you right counsel for the person and faith for his situation.

Normally you will pray in English, but there will be times when you use the gift of tongues during your prayer time—perhaps when you need some specific guidance or when you want to intercede for an unknown situation. Sometimes an interpretation will follow your prayer in tongues.

When you pray, remember that prayer is *two-way* communication; there will be times when you want to listen. Expect to hear the Lord speak into your heart—Jesus said you would (Jn 10:4).

Keep a notebook and record the things which God says to you and the ways he answers prayer in your life, both in your family and in connection with the members of your house group. God's plans and purposes are exciting, and your notebook will be a constant reminder to you of what he is doing; this will build up your faith for what you want to ask him *now*. Look back in your notebook when you are tempted to feel discouraged, and begin to praise God afresh for his faithfulness, love and power. Listen to tapes (the car is a good place for this if you drive to work) and try to fit in some reading of books which will build up your faith.

Sometimes you will be seeking God's guidance as you pray. If you are not sure that you have heard him, wait. The Holy Spirit is persistent; he will not let you forget what he wants you to hear, but will gently speak to you again until you are certain of his voice and at peace in what he is saying to you. Expect confirmation, too, from other sources; God will often confirm his individual word to you through prayer, prophecy, interpretation of tongues or ministry when you are in the larger congregation of believers. If God speaks to you about taking some specific action, check it out with others as necessary; true guidance from God will be confirmed in your heart and in the hearts of others by the peace of God (see Philippians 4:6–7 and Colossians 3:15).

As you put these things into practice in your own prayer life, you will be able to share them with your house group; together you will share the adventure of seeing God answer in unmistakable ways when you pray.

Fitting your prayer time into your lifestyle

Depending on your family and your daily routine, you will need to work out the best time to pray. The traditional 'first thing in the morning' is not the best time for everyone, especially if you have a baby who does not yet know that nights are for sleeping! It is better to decide on a certain time—say, three times a week—than to try and fit in time every day 'against the clock'. The Lord knows your time schedule, and living in fellowship with him in a relaxed manner is far better than planning to fit in a prayer time every day whatever happens and then feeling constantly condemned because you fail to do it. To aim for three times a week is better. Be at peace in your heart regarding your personal prayer plan; make it realistic according to your life-style and then keep to it as far as possible. Be disciplined, but not legalistic.

You and your wife will want to pray together about family and house-group matters, and it is important that you do so. You may find it helpful to pray together each evening before bed, if you are not too tired; or on one specific evening a week, perhaps the day before (or after) the house group meets in your home. Find a time when you are both able to give yourselves freely to prayer, even if only for a short while.

Prayer in the house group

Prayer in the house group will usually take the form of intercessory prayer; you will be presenting specific requests to God about people and situations. Perhaps the elders have asked the house groups to pray for a person in difficulties; or the church may be having a special outreach meeting; perhaps the young people are going on a weekend retreat; or there may be a problem with one of the Sunday School children. Or perhaps all the house groups have been asked to pray specifically for the local area this week—a well-known medium is conducting a public seance in the town hall on Saturday night and the leaders of the church have asked every house group to spend their evening praying against this in a very definite way.

It may be that you are going to pray just for your own house group's concerns on a particular evening. Heather and Jill have a friend at college who is showing a real interest in the Christian faith; she is coming to church with them for the first time on Sunday. Brian and Pat's youngest child, Peter, is taking a long time to recover from a bad bout of pneumonia and they have asked the group to pray for him. Bob is having problems at home—his mother is baffled by the fact that he is now coming to church and enjoying it, not just once but *twice* on a Sunday; and he is reading the Bible as well! He has also stopped swearing. She is suspicious and puzzled. Bob wants the house group to pray for her; he doesn't feel it's quite time yet to ask her to come to church, but he wants to help her understand what has happened to him. John has earache and wants the group to pray for healing for him.

It is obvious that there are many different prayer concerns for your house group to be tackling at various times. But it is always a good idea for you, as leader, to decide on a 'plan of campaign' to ensure that the prayer evening is a very positive time for your house group.

Have clear prayer topics

When you come together, tell the house group exactly what you are going to be praying about. There may be several items—share any necessary details about each one.

Begin with worship

Before you begin to pray, it is good to have a short time of worship, which will focus the hearts of people on God and allow faith to rise in their hearts. However, worship should not continue for more than ten minutes or a quarter of an hour; you have come together for specific, intercessory prayer.

Take one subject at a time

Don't pray for several matters together; take them one at a time. Tell the group which matter you are going to pray about now, then spend a few minutes silently waiting on God as a group before you pray. Often God will begin to direct your praying as you wait in his presence. Later, you will need to be sensitive to the leading of the Spirit in knowing when it is time to finish praying for that particular matter and move on to the next.

Encourage participation

Encourage each person in the group to take part, even if it is only a sentence or two of prayer. Point out that it is perfectly in order to pray for what someone else has already prayed—after all, you are concentrating on prayer for the same thing!

Be sensitive to the Holy Spirit

Be open to the Holy Spirit giving direction while you are praying. It may be that someone will receive a word of knowledge or wisdom concerning the situation for which you are praying (see 1 Corinthians 12:8). One or two in the group may be given faith to lay hands on John and pray in the name of Jesus for the healing of his ear. Someone may be given a vision or picture which throws light upon a problem. A prophecy may be given, or someone may be led to read aloud a passage of Scripture which brings some clarity into a situation. You, as leader, will need to hold together all that happens and to close the session of prayer when it is time to do so. Then sum up for the group all that has come from the prayer time, and decide on any action that may need to be taken by you or someone else in the group. For instance, you may have been praying for the unconverted husband of someone in the group. God may have impressed on the group during prayer that they need to take a real interest in the husband as a person, and to invite him to their homes with his wife rather than just praying for him. God may have shown someone else that this man feels lonely and needs his wife's love and company, whereas she has been under the impression that he doesn't want her around so much since she became a Christian. Both the group and the wife will have to take some action after this prayer session!

Prayer warfare

There will be times when your praying will be spiritual warfare. You will need to take a specific stand against the activity of Satan in the life of a member of the group or someone else in the church; or against a situation where Satan is very evidently causing real hindrance to the work of Christ or the spread of the gospel in your locality.

At times it will be right for you to ask the whole group to stand together and pray aloud in tongues. At other times it will be necessary to resist and rebuke Satan and his principalities and powers, using the authority that Christ has given the church to do this.

You may have been praying about a situation for some time when suddenly you all feel that a breakthrough has come—that a victory has been won, or something definite has been accomplished. Then you can praise God, even if you do not know exactly what has happened in the situation.

The whole matter of spiritual warfare is outside the scope of this book, but you should give yourself to learning as much as you can about this important aspect of prayer. We are told in 1 John 3:8 that the purpose of Jesus' coming was to destroy the devil's work. We must be willing and ready for him to use us for this. The well-known passage in Ephesians 6:10–18 speaks of putting on armour, struggling, resisting and standing firm. The verbs are all plural; it is a corporate battle. Call your house group to war!

Look for results

When you have a prayer evening in your house group it is a good idea to record your prayer topics in a notebook—requests, dated, on the left-hand pages and answers, dated, on the right-hand pages. You may have to pray consistently for a long time about some matters, but keep trusting God. There was immense joy in one of our house groups when, after a year of constant prayer, the husband of one of the members gave his life to the Lord in middle age. He is growing rapidly in the Christian faith; and on two occasions recently, when the leader had to be away, he actually led the house group which had prayed him into the kingdom of God. Worth recording in a notebook!

If you have been praying in response to a prayer request from the elders of the church, make sure you feed back the results, or any further news, to your group. When you have been engaging in fervent prayer for someone it is discouraging if you do not hear whether that prayer has been answered or whether you should continue to pray.

Spontaneous praying

There will be some house-group evenings when you will not necessarily have planned a prayer time, but prayer will just happen. Perhaps someone will arrive at house group feeling worried and upset about something, or somebody has been made redundant unexpectedly, or one of the young people in the group has a difficult home situation. On these occasions the group will want to pray for the person concerned and show them love and support. There may be times when the group will want to pray for you and your wife, if they sense (or you tell them) that you are feeling particularly tired or under pressure.

Prayer is communication with God

We have a mighty God who delights to answer the prayers of a people who are walking in fellowship with him and praying according to his will. Prayer is communication with him—encourage your group to get excited about it!

9

Counselling individuals in the house group

People are individuals and they will have their own very personal needs, problems and difficulties as well as their own goals, aspirations and victories. Most of the time you will be in a group context with your house-group members, but there will be times when you will be asked for help, counsel or advice by individuals.

Group leaders and wives will obviously not all have the same ability or experience to help people, and this chapter will not turn you into an expert counsellor or pastor in one easy step. But you will need to know something about helping people on a one-to-one basis; and you will also want to know when you need to call in your minister or elders. We hope that this chapter will help to give you an understanding of the kind of needs likely to arise within your group and how to give counsel and help to people.

The house group will reveal needs

You will find that when Christians are brought into the kind of loving and caring relationships which we have been describing in this book, two things will happen. Firstly, people will be helped. There are many people who have very big hurts as a result of things which have happened in their past. Many will never have known what it is to be genuinely loved and cared for, nor will they have been in a situation where they can lower their defences and just be themselves. Without any special ministry or counsel the fact of just belonging, being accepted and receiving your shepherding care is going to do a deep healing work within them. You will see the truth of Jesus' observation in Matthew 9:36, when he saw the crowds as sheep without a shepherd.

The second thing you will notice may seem at first sight to be a contradiction of this: people's needs will be revealed. The very atmosphere of love and care which heals also highlights needs. That, of course, is what God wants in order that the problems can be solved. (*Your* initial reaction may be one of dismay unless you understand this!) You will find that deep hurts, prejudices, fears, wrong attitudes, etc., which have been buried or carefully controlled will begin to surface. You may notice that Bill never joins in a time of laughter or fun; that Paul reacts very strongly when his viewpoint is contradicted; that Janet may retreat into her shell whenever the group begins a time of sharing on a personal level; that Robert has to monopolize every conversation; or that Pam is very, very fearful. Obviously you won't want to jump in right away; but if these attitudes persist some action and help is needed. At times you will have to take the initiative—if, for instance, a situation should arise where a damaging attitude or reaction causes real hurt to somebody—but you will find that as people begin to value and appreciate you and your wife they will want to talk over their needs and problems with you. The problems won't all be deep counselling affairs; perhaps advice is needed about changing a job, some opportunity for service in the church or a family situation. However, there will inevitably be needs and problems that are deeper and more fundamental. The rest of this chapter is concerned with these needs.

Some general principles

Let's imagine a situation. Last Sunday Bill asked you if he could come and have a chat with you this week as he has a problem he wants to share. It's now Friday evening and Bill is sitting in your front room rather nervously shuffling his feet. You and your wife have prayed several times during the week about Bill, but now the moment has arrived (the first time you've been in this situation) you feel even more nervous than Bill! What do you do? The Scriptures don't give us a formula or a technique, but the following steps will enable you to understand and help Bill or whoever it may be.

Rely upon the Holy Spirit

It is helpful in most cases to say at the beginning, 'Bill, before you share your problem let's ask God to give us his wisdom and knowledge. The Holy Spirit is the great counsellor and we can trust him.' Right away both you and Bill have established the fact that it is more than just human wisdom and experience that is needed (and will be received). Rely upon God to give you wisdom, insight and understanding. Expect God, too, to give you utterances of wisdom and words of knowledge if these are necessary (1 Cor 12:8).

Listen to people

Most of us are not very good listeners. You will need to learn to listen to Bill. He may not come straight to the point. You may have to help him out. 'Bill, I can see you're having difficulty sharing this need. I just want you to know that you are doing the right thing in sharing it.' Listening is not just on the human level, either. Learn to listen to God at the same time. 'Lord, what Bill is sharing doesn't seem to be everything; there are deeper issues here. Should I press him about these or leave it for another time?' It is also very important that you ask questions so that you really understand the problem. It is no good trying to give help if you haven't understood the need. Some problems are simple and straightforward, but others will be complex and will need long-term help. Some may be beyond your ability to help and you will need to say to Bill, 'I think we should chat to the elders about this—would you like me to fix that up for you?' But assuming that is not necessary, let's look at how you should proceed.

Find God's solution

Individual problems need individual answers. As you and the person you are helping seek God together he will show you specific ways in which that person can be helped. We could not begin to cover all the possibilities, but we will look at the broad areas of need and see how to work toward specific solutions in the lives of individual people.

Helping a person to understand the truth

Often you will find that people have problems because they don't fully understand what has been happening. New Christians are often in trouble over this. They find that they are suddenly facing temptation and the attacks of Satan (though they may not describe it in those words). They are very worried and wonder what has happened; you will need to teach them.

It may be that some people have begun to see the effect of Christian love within the family of God's people; this may bring back memories of a childhood experience of neglect, misunderstanding or lack of affection. Those who have experienced this in childhood often start to blame themselves—especially if they feel they were not wanted. Their self-image may be very low. They will need to be carefully shown from the Scriptures that God wanted them (Eph 1:4; 2 Thess 2:13); that God knew all about that difficult childhood and he is able to make it work for good (Rom 8:28). You will certainly need to pray for them and bring them to a place of real faith in God's word.

Some may be prey to the subtle lies of the devil about

themselves, others and even God himself. Satan is the 'father of lies' (Jn 8:44) and he seeks to fill our minds with untruth, particularly with regard to God. Some people cannot think of God as very much more than a stern head-master figure; consequently their whole Christian life of prayer, worship, joy, etc., is affected. You will need to show them where that lie comes from. They will need to understand how Satan operates and learn not to receive and nurture (or become a 'mother' to) those lies, but to believe the truth. Jesus is *the* truth and he fully reveals the character of God the Father.

Helping a person face up to his responsibilities

God doesn't forgive excuses, only sin that has been con-fessed! Often you will have to help people face up to the responsibility of their actions. This is never easy; we are all adept at 'passing the buck'. Look at Genesis 3:11–12, Exodus 32:21–24 and 1 Samuel 13:7–14 and see how Adam, Aaron and Saul all tried it. The basis of these excuses was, 'I couldn't help it'. The fact is, of course, we *can* help it; the fact is that we are foolish, or disobedient or lazy. For many, many people the doorway to victory is to face up to their responsibilities. You will need to help them do this.

Bob may come to you with a problem about buying pornographic magazines. 'I can't help it—I just see them in the shop and buy them.' It's possible that there are other factors involved, but it may simply be that he needs to face up to the fact that for several years he has just been excusing himself. Now that he is a believer he needs to recognize that reading pornographic magazines is harmful and wrong; he must confess it to God, repent and seek the help of the Holy Spirit. Note that it is 'by the Spirit you put to death the misdeeds of the body' (Rom 8:13). Part of the 'putting to death' for Bob will mean not going into that shop again.

Paul may come to you because of financial problems; he has had the Electricity Board's final demand and has no money to pay. 'What shall I do?' he asks. You will need to ask, 'How is it you can't pay? You earn a good salary.' 'Well, I've never been able to manage money—I'm afraid it just seems to burn a hole in my pocket!' You will have to weigh carefully whether this is something you can handle or whether the minister or elders should take over. (You would be wise to share it with them in any case.) Paul will probably need some short-term financial help, but the bigger problem is helping him organize his finances. The best thing might be to see if the Electricity Board can extend the period of payment. Then you can get Paul to face up to the responsibility of proper budgeting (including teaching on tithing, for he may be treating that in the same casual manner). You, or someone else who is in a similar income bracket to Paul and who has similar responsibilities, may need to spend several evenings with both Paul and Pam if this is a constant difficulty.

As with all ministry, helping people face up to responsibility must be done out of genuine love. Another prerequisite, according to Galatians 6:1, is gentleness. Speaking the truth in love (Eph 4:15) does not mean that we should not be firm and definite, but it does mean that we should definitely not be judgemental. Some people come to a point of real despair over their failures and mistakes. They need to know that you care about them and will not only seek God's answer for them but will constantly and lovingly encourage them until they come into victory. Not one of us can afford to judge another. The apostle Paul, a leader 'par excellence', sums up the right attitude for a leader in 1 Corinthians 9:27.

Setting clear goals

If a person has a problem because he has been neglecting certain vital matters or indulging in wrong attitudes or actions, the obvious answer is to establish new and right patterns of thinking and behaviour. Because we are 'in

Christ' we can 'put off' things which belong to the old life and 'put on' things which belong to the new. To do so requires *action*. For instance, Jill may frequently have problems in certain areas because she hardly ever has a regular time of prayer and fellowship with God. Asking God's forgiveness will not put things right. Setting a goal will! She will need you to help her see how to organize her time. She may not know how to fellowship with God or read the Scriptures with understanding; again, you will need to help her see how important this is and give her some specific help—perhaps linking her with someone who can spend some time with her regularly to encourage her and pray with her.

Bob's problem, mentioned earlier, is one of those referred to by Paul in his second letter to Timothy. Note Paul's counsel in 2 Timothy 2:22, from which there are three immediate goals you can give Bob—to flee from evil desires, to pursue righteousness and to get alongside Christians who will help him.

Identifying the real difficulty

You will find that very few problems are isolated; they are usually part of a whole pattern of life. Brian comes to you with his problem. It looms very large in his thinking and seems to be *the* great need in his life. Let's say that the problem is an acute guilt complex. When you begin to ask him about it, it is evident that other areas of his life are being affected by it. He is unable to sleep. He is unable to worship freely. As you probe further you discover that he is always late for work, he is behind in several hire purchase payments, has failed to do a number of urgent household repairs (which is not helping his relationship with his wife), and has failed to keep several promises made to his children (which is not helping his relationship with them, either). So it is evident that his problem of guilt is caused by the fact that his rather undisciplined and thoughtless way of life is catching up with him! The fact is that our actions are inter-related, and Brian needs some help in organizing his life better. Helping him to see the cause of the problem will probably be part of the cure.

In this chapter we have done no more than give some guidelines. Most of the situations mentioned are not outside the scope of the majority of house-group leaders, bearing in mind that they will not all happen at once! But there may be people whom you realize are not being helped by normal counselling; however much you seek to bring them to a place of faith in God's provision, they just do not seem to come to a place of appropriation and victory. In these cases you must share the matter with your elders. If you suspect that someone has been involved in any occult practices in the past or is troubled by the demonic, your elders will need to know so that appropriate action may be taken to help the person. Sometimes a traumatic occurrence during childhood can open a 'door' in someone's life to the entrance and activity of evil spirits. Even though that person has subsequently come into new life in Christ, deliverance ministry will be needed before he can hope to gain victory over his problems. This kind of need is evidenced in a variety of ways: habitual failure in certain areas of life; compulsive attitudes or behaviour; a tendency to withdraw from people; inability to communicate or relate adequately; extreme defensiveness or aggression; insecurity and a low self-image which persists in spite of scriptural teaching; and persistent inability to appropriate the truths of Scripture. Any of these characteristics in the life of a person may indicate a need for deliverance ministry. If, after counselling a person, you feel that this is a possibility you should communicate the matter immediately to your minister or elders and let them take it from there.

Some counselling situations you may face

Having read through the chapter so far, think carefully about how you would help someone who has a problem in the following areas:

(a) depression (refer to Psalm 42 and Philippians 4:4–8),
(b) guilt (refer to Psalm 32, Psalm 51 and 1 John 1),
(c) Husband/wife relationships (look at Ephesians 5 and 1 Peter 3),
(d) difficulties in the use of spiritual gifts (look at 1 Corinthians 12 and 14).

Try some role play here—get your wife to be the person with the problem, and the ensuing discussion may help you when the *real* person with the problem comes along at a later date.

Counselling the opposite sex

Be careful when counselling female members of your house group. It is not usually a good idea to do this on your own; neither is it a good idea for you to visit, for counselling purposes, single women living on their own. The ideal situation is for women who need help or counsel to come and talk to you *and your wife* in your own home. It is, of course, right that the women in your house group should trust your leadership and turn to you for help, but you need to remember that women on their own may be emotionally vulnerable. Satan would love to bring you into temptation and ruin your reputation or that of your church. Don't give him the opportunity.

Confidentiality is important

The members of your house group should know that when they share a personal problem or difficulty with you it will not be shared with anyone else. The only exception to this is the eldership of the church; it may be necessary at times to communicate the problem to them in order for the person to receive further help or guidance. However, your group members should know that there is no possibility of their private conversation with you being repeated in any other company than the eldership; they should be able to trust you, and you and your wife must be careful to honour that trust. You should make it clear that you do not have secrets from your wife; this puts you both under a strain and is not advisable, especially as you and your wife are 'one flesh'. But reassure those who come for counsel that you will both keep their confidence.

God wants free people

It should be obvious by now that one of the reasons why God has been impressing upon the church the need for smaller, sharing and caring groups is because it is necessary for people to be helped through their personal problems and spiritual 'hang-ups'. The result will be a group of people who know how to pray with authority because Satan has no foothold in their lives; a group of people who know how to love and care for each other, and how to receive new Christians and help them grow in the faith; and a group of people who are willing and glad to share the truth that has set them free.

10

Dealing with difficult people in the house group

We are not going to discuss serious personality problems in this chapter. People with this kind of difficulty usually need skilled help. In our experience it is unwise for a person with a serious problem to be put directly into a house group; he will demand an excessive amount of the leader's time and attention and may well 'take over' or disrupt the group meeting. At the very least he will probably not be able to relate properly with other members of the group. It is better if he meets with one of the elders on a regular basis while receiving any other necessary help. Eventually it will become apparent whether or not he is ready for a house group.

In this chapter we shall be looking at the 'normal' range of difficult people you as leader are likely to encounter. Remember, they will not all be in your group at the same time! Remember, too, that there are no 'problem people'. There are people who have problems, and those who are willing and open to God can find solutions to their problems and difficulties. Encourage them in this and assure them of your love and commitment. People with problems need the love and care of their leader and their house group. But they can be a great drain on the leader's strength if the problems continue indefinitely. This chapter aims to help you see the causes behind some of the problems people have, and some of the steps towards resolving the difficulties.

Start with yourself

'All the world is queer, save thee and me, and even thou art a little queer', wrote Robert Owen in the eighteenth century. Every person is an individual, and there are times when your particular personality may clash with that of someone in your group who is very different. This may lead to a communication problem; you may find the person 'difficult' because you do not relate easily with him. He may be quiet and shy, while you are outgoing and friendly—or the reverse may be the case. Perhaps you have been involved in a broken relationship with someone outside your house group; this can affect your ability to relate to other people who have similar personalities to that person. Broken relationships are a serious matter in the kingdom of God, particularly for those in leadership. As Arthur Wallis puts it, 'A dislocated shoulder means an arm which is non-functional' (*Restoration* Mar/Apr 1981). Any relationship failure which continues *because you do not seek to put it right* is sin.

When you have checked this out in your own life and know yourself to be clear of any broken relationship on your part, go on to look at your house group. Is there any member to whom you find it hard to relate? Ask yourself whether the reason lies with you rather than with the other person. Are you afraid that he will not fully accept you as leader? Do you feel inadequate in the face of his greater intellectual ability? Do you have a critical or judgemental attitude towards him which is preventing any real contact and fellowship?

Let God deal with your inner attitudes. If you are critical and judgemental you are disobeying God; you are also unable to assess the other person accurately (see Matthew 7:3–5). You need to have a forbearing spirit. Jesus' team of apostles was composed of men who were completely different in temperament and approach, but it was their *relationship with Jesus* which held them together and enabled them to overcome superficial differences.

If you find that your relationships with people are affected by their accent, their income, their taste in clothes or their IQ, it would be helpful to read through chapter 2 of the epistle of James. It is clear from this chapter that favouritism can hinder your life and leadership. Jesus committed himself to his apostles because he knew *what they could become through the power of God*. We must have that same attitude.

If you have difficulty in relating to someone in your group because of fear or inadequacy, read carefully through Romans 12 and link it with 1 Peter 4:10. You might find it useful to read again the sections in chapter 3 dealing with 'security' and 'self-image'. Remember that *God* has put you in leadership of your group.

Stress can cause a temporary problem

There will be times when someone may be uncharacter-istically 'difficult', because he is under stress. You should recognize this and offer support. Your example, too, will help. If you and your wife can remain calm and trusting in God through your own crisis situation of a child's serious illness, a problem at work or a seemingly interminable delay in house purchase, then the members of your group will be encouraged to do the same. Stress and pressure in the life of a Christian needs to be honestly faced and tackled. God will often use the pressures that come into our lives to help us learn dependence upon him and how to help others (see 2 Corinthians 1:1–10). You may find it helpful to read *Triumphing Under Stress* by Peter Thompson.

Those who are silent and withdrawn

There is a difference between a 'quiet' person and a person who is silent and withdrawn. Someone who is quiet may not necessarily be shy and insecure—he may be perfectly happy and involved in all that is happening. A quiet person who feels accepted and loved by the group will eventually begin to participate and respond in a greater measure than before; but it is a good thing for you to chat to him fairly frequently at times other than the group meeting to check that things are going well with him—the quiet ones probably will not seek you out so readily when they need help! However, the person who is very silent and withdrawn, and who does not respond to or relate easily with you and the others in the group may well have a problem. You will need to get to know him outside the group meeting and seek to communicate love and acceptance to him in a very definite way. His reluctance to open up may be due to fear of rejection and this can be the result of bad experiences going back as far as early childhood. If he does not respond eventually to the loving care and commitment of you and your wife it may be necessary for one of the elders to see him. In some cases this kind of deeply-felt rejection is caused by a demonic spirit and the person may need deliverance ministry.

Another person may be quiet and withdrawn because he does not want to reveal his ignorance, especially about spiritual matters! He may even feel that his opinions are not worth anything. Someone like this is often insecure and unsure of his place in the group. Again love, care and interest are vital if he is to gain the confidence to 'come out of his shell'.

Those who are noisy and talkative

A person who is constantly and disruptively loud and talkative in the house group is communicating the fact that he urgently needs to be noticed. This may stem from a childhood when he was continually silenced or compared unfavourably with a brother or sister, and may mean that he has problems of insecurity with which he will need help. Make sure he *is* noticed, but be firm and insist that he is quiet when you ask him to be quiet.

A strong person who is talkative can tend to dominate

the group, and if he is articulate and strongly opinionated he can 'upstage' everybody else, including you! You will need to talk to him about this, pointing out that the quieter members of the group can feel threatened by his behaviour and that they also need opportunities to speak and share in the group. Try getting the talkative person to prepare and lead a discussion group or Bible study occasionally; it may be profitable for him and for the rest of the group to 'channel' his vocal energy in this way.

Those who are very traditional

These will usually be older folk who have been Christians for many years. They may welcome new and abundant life in the church but have difficulty coming to terms with some of the outworking of this life—young people who come to church in jeans, Christians who don't keep Sunday in the same strict way as they do, and even new translations of the Bible! Those who truly love the Lord and his word will be open to you gently sharing Scriptures with them which will help them to differentiate between traditional legalism and biblical truth. 'Keeping the Sabbath day holy' should not be translated 'Don't go swimming on Sunday afternoons'.

Those who are rigid in their outlook are harder to deal with. Share their need privately with the other members of the house group and determine together to pray for them and love them until their hearts are melted. This may take time, and certainly patience and tolerance will be needed.

Those who are argumentative

A person who continually argues with you or challenges your statements in the group will cause disruption and disharmony (to say nothing of wasting time!) if he or she is allowed to continue. You need to talk to him privately and ascertain whether he is a rebel or a genuine seeker after truth. If he is the latter, you will help him most by spending time with him and getting to know him; talk to him about the unhelpfulness of arguing during the group meeting and show him the scriptures in Ephesians 4:29 and James 1:19–20. Assure him that you really want to help him learn and grow as a Christian, and let him borrow or buy books which will teach him truth and doctrine. A book such as *Know the Truth* by Bruce Milne will probably make it unnecessary for him to bring all his doctrinal arguments to the house-group meeting. Arrange with him to talk after the meeting if he has problems with something you say in group, unless he can learn to discuss rather than argue; there may be times when the whole group could be helped by a question or a query discussed in a positive way.

If a person is continually arguing because he is rebellious it is a much more serious matter. Argument can cause real distress and discord in a house group, and a habitual rebel should be reported to the elders for them to take action. This kind of rebellion is unlikely to happen in a house group which is composed of people who have come into the group in commitment to the church and the elders, but it is necessary for leaders to be aware of the possibility.

Sometimes a person is argumentative because he feels defensive about the subject under discussion; he may have a problem or difficulty in that area and so reacts with self-defence and argument when the subject comes up. If you feel that this is the cause, the best way of dealing with it is to talk to the person afterwards and gently seek to help him open up about his personal difficulty. You could say something like, 'Brian, I sensed that your strong reaction when we were discussing personal communication tonight indicates that a sore spot was touched. Am I right? Would you like to talk about it?'

Those who will not be serious

Someone who has a reputation as a 'clown' can be very disruptive if he will never stop being a comic. You will need to talk to him on his own and find out why he always wants to be funny. He may feel he is no good at anything else, in which case you will need to help him develop other talents. Sometimes a person like this can be greatly helped by having the responsibility of 'discipling' a younger Christian.

Someone who will never be serious with you may have difficulties in relating to you as a leader—particularly if he knew you before you came into leadership. If this is the case you must explain to him how much you need his help and co-operation in the group.

Those who cannot make strong relationships

There may be someone in your group who seems unable to make relationships with others except on a very superficial level. This may be because he does not know how to; perhaps he has only recently become a Christian and open, loving relationships are not something he has ever experienced before—and therefore does not quite know how to handle! This may also be true of a very 'traditional' Christian who has newly received the baptism in the Spirit. You will need to show him from the Scriptures that believers are to be one in heart and mind and to share their lives with one another at a deep and honest level (Acts 4:32). Encourage him to learn to love, and show him from 1 Thessalonians 3:12 and 4:9 that the Lord is very willing to teach him. The love, affection and care shown to him by you and the group will be a real-life demonstration of the kind of relationship possible between Christians.

Sometimes fear will prevent a person making deep relationships—fear of revealing too much of himself in case people reject him. He may feel like the person quoted in John Powell's book *Why Am I Afraid to Tell You Who I Am?* who said, 'I am afraid to tell you who I am because, if I tell you who I am, you may not like who I am, and it's all that I have.' Rejection, as we said earlier, can be such a serious problem in a person's life that deliverance ministry is needed before that person can begin to relate on any deep level with his brothers and sisters in Christ.

A positive and helpful way to foster good relationships in the house group is to use a 'one-to-one' system which changes every three months. Everyone in the group is linked to another person in the group, and for three months they make it their aim to get to know their 'other half' really well. During this time they should a) have a meal together on a regular basis, b) pray together once a week, and c) share personal needs as they arise. With some pairs it will take longer, and one half of the pair may have to work harder at the beginning, but by the end of the three months there should be a good relationship formed which will help them to build another good relationship over the next three months with the next person. There are ways of varying this system, and you will know which is best for your particular house group. You may prefer to have 'getting-to-know-you' groups of three or four, but the one-to-one way may be better for helping those who find it difficult to make relationships.

Those who are super-spiritual

Super-spiritual people are often those who are fearful of being themselves—before God or anyone else! They feel somehow that God is not too keen on his people being human; that he much prefers them to be at prayer than at a football match, or at a mid-week meeting than a meal together. They need to be shown that when we are 'in Christ' our whole lives are lived in him; that he wants us to enjoy ourselves with our families and friends; that we can shout for Brighton and Hove Albion at a football match as loudly as we shout 'Hallelujah!' in a praise meeting and still be pleasing to God.

A super-spiritual person may be 'unreal' in his praying in the group. This sense of unreality can mean that he has problems in his life which have not been brought into the open and he is using the super-spiritual mask to cover up the unacceptable (to him) face beneath. He needs to be gently shown that his problems are much more acceptable than his 'spiritual' mask; that God and the group can love and accept a person, not a pretence, and that if he can only bring himself to be real and open about himself and his failings he will become secure and know himself to be accepted on a real and honest basis.

Those who are negative

Someone who is always negative in his attitudes is an unhelpful member in the house group. Negative attitudes are very catching and they militate against faith. These attitudes may have been learned from parents in early childhood, and the person needs to be encouraged to see that he is a new person in Christ and can now develop a more scriptural and positive response to situations. Negative people need love and acceptance, but they also need to face up to what they are doing and the effect that it can have upon people in the group. One helpful approach may be to get a very negative person to study the life of Jesus with real attention, and help him to see how positive Jesus was in every situation (particularly when facing the cross and when dealing with the matter of Peter's denial) and how committed to his Father's will. Encourage the negative person to review God's answers to prayer, and ask him not to voice negative responses in the group but to come and talk with you about how he feels.

Those who won't receive your counsel

Let's consider the following situation…you have talked with a person about a problem and have counselled him to take a particular course of action or to aim for some specific goal. It eventually becomes obvious that he has ignored your counsel and is making no effort to achieve the goal set.

What should you do? First, make sure that he has had ample time to put your counsel into operation. He may have been prevented by illness, absence or something else. If you are sure that this is not the case, then you need to see him and bring the matter out into the open. He may tell you that he has legitimate reason for failing to act on your counsel. Perhaps he feels that the circumstances make it impossible (for example, a marital problem where his wife is unwilling to co-operate in working at the situation). He may feel that it can be left indefinitely—that he will get round to it 'sometime'. Perhaps he feels that the effort is too much, that growth is not *that* important. It may even be that he is rejecting your leadership and has no intention of following your counsel. You will need to elicit the reasons behind his failure to act and then give him real encouragement to get on with it, assuring him of your support and prayer. If no progress is subsequently made it may be necessary to talk the matter over with the elders.

Those who do not grow

'Nothing changes here' seems to be the watchword for some people. They never change; continually predictable in their opinions and reactions, never trying anything new or leaving the old familiar pathways and routines. Lack of growth (assuming that good nourishment is being provided!) usually stems from lack of commitment. The person who is uncommitted to the Lord, to his leaders and to his brothers and sisters in Christ has no motivation for growth or change. If you are sure that this is the cause, the person must be faced up with it. There is need for real, honest and loving confrontation.

A positive approach

We do not mean this chapter to discourage you, and we do not want to major on problems. Leading a house group means tremendous joy and encouragement as you see people learning and growing in love and commitment to the Lord, to you and to one another. But *sometimes some* people behave in ways which we do not understand, and we hope that this chapter will help you to see ways of bringing these people through to a better understanding of themselves and of the power of God to change them.

I I

Assessing progress in the house group

The mother who takes her baby to the clinic to be weighed, the father who queues up at a school parents' evening to see his son's maths teacher, the enthusiastic six-year-old who digs up his daffodil bulb to see how much it has grown are all interested in one thing: progress. The apostle writing to the Hebrews is talking about progress—or lack of it—when he tells them that they are 'slow to learn' (Heb 5:11). He goes on to say that they have made so little progress as Christians that they are like babies drinking milk instead of mature adults who are able to eat meat. He challenges them to leave the elementary teachings of Jesus, which should be firmly built as a foundation into their lives, and move on towards the goal of maturity (Heb 6:1).

Progress is made by setting goals; achieved goals are the measure of progress. If you can help the members of your house group to learn to set goals for themselves and work towards achieving those goals, you will have helped them take an enormous step towards maturity as people, both spiritually and emotionally.

It is a good idea, at fairly long intervals, to have a group 'assessment evening' when each person in the group is given an opportunity to assess his or her progress. The beginning of a new year is a good time for this, or a time when the group is together for a day or a weekend. A session on 'What progress have I made this year?' could be followed by one on 'What are my goals for the coming year?'

Use a questionnaire

Start the evening with coffee and chat, then give everyone a list of questions. This can be done verbally with you reading out each question and allowing five minutes or so for the answer to be written down; or you can simply give people the list of questions and paper for their answers and announce that they can have half an hour to complete it. (It may be wise for people to turn their chairs at an angle away from one another while they complete the questions; this prevents distractions or inadvertent viewing of other people's answers.) The main question, 'What progress have I made as a person during this past year?', can be dealt with by focusing on different areas. Have I grown in my *spiritual life*? Do I know God better than I did a year ago? Am I dealing with sin in my life, or accommodating it? Have I grown in my *emotional life*? Am I more self-controlled than I was a year ago? Am I learning to conquer my shyness? Have I grown in my *relationships*? Am I building positive friendships? Am I avoiding anyone? If so, why? Have I increased in my *abilities*? Have I improved at skills I already possess? Have I learned any new skills this year?

Once the questionnaire has been completed, you may find it helpful to lead into a time of sharing your answers and talking about them together. However, some groups may not feel comfortable with this. It may be better for all the papers to be handed in and for the leader to sum up a 'collective assessment' of the group the following week, leading into a discussion on 'What are my goals for the next year?' You will know which is the best approach for your group. If there are those who feel that they have made very little progress, you will need to encourage them and remind them of the assurance in Philippians 1:6 that God *will* complete the work he has begun in each of his children.

Goals are important

It is important to follow an assessment of progress with new goals, and you can discuss with your group various goals which each person can apply according to his own needs. For instance, Bob wants to grow in his knowledge of the Bible. A good goal for him would, perhaps, be to read through the Bible in a year following a reading plan. He'll need some encouragement to stick at this, and it would be helpful if someone else with the same 'goal' could do it too so they could encourage each other. Janet knows that she needs to grow in the area of making friendships. A good goal for her would be to get to know two new people really well during the coming year. Paul and Pam have both realized how few Christian books they read, and want to make a real effort here. Their goal could be to read at least four Christian books during the year. They may need some help in finding books that they will really enjoy and that will help them grow in their Christian life. These are all individual goals, but the group as a whole has expressed a real desire to grow in *faith*. Faith needs to be exercised and stretched if it is to increase, so there is a need to get to grips with specific prayer targets to enable the group's faith to be tested and strengthened. Every answered prayer will bring an increase of faith for the next one!

Keep a private record

It will be helpful if you, as leader, keep a (private!) record of each individual in your group. This can be done in a large notebook, using a page for each person. Details about each person can go on his or her page; not just family details, but details of his gifts and abilities, his spiritual progress and any specific needs. This will help you to pray intelligently for each person in your group, and to help them decide on their personal goals. If you are in a church where there is no commitment group or class prior to house-group membership, your goals for each individual may be basic to his Christian growth. You will need to show him the need for baptism in water and in the Holy Spirit; he will need to learn how to be free in worship; and how to relate to his new brothers and sisters as well as how to witness to his family and work-mates. All these areas of progress can be noted in your private record-book, and it will be useful to you when your pastors or elders want to talk with you (as they should on a regular basis) about the health and progress of your house group and of its individual members.

Provide the means for progress

The house group must provide opportunities for growth and progress, and your planning of a varied programme for your group will ensure that this happens. Worship, which should form part of your evening nearly every week, will bring about spiritual growth in those who give themselves to it. Those who 'behold the glory of the Lord', according to 2 Corinthians 3:18, are 'transformed into his likeness'. Worship is not only something which God requires of us, but it is also vital to Christian growth.

Teaching is also very important; at least one good teaching session a month will help the members of your house group grow in their knowledge of the Scriptures and of their application to life. An evening spent discussing and applying the previous Sunday's ministry will do the same. A testimony or 'sharing' evening will help people learn to be open about their needs and experiences. An evening of prayer and intercession will help them learn to care for one another and bring one another to God for his power to be released in their lives. An evening spent decorating someone's front room or clearing the garden will teach them practical care and consideration—that 'faith by itself, if it is not accompanied by action, is dead' (Jas 2:17). A meal together, ending with communion or breaking of bread, will help them learn to relax together and enjoy one another's company in the presence of God. A games evening (especially if Monopoly is included!) will reveal character in a remarkable way, and thus indicate possible areas where progress is needed. A music or record evening, with its inevitable 'mix' of tastes, will give opportunity for learning to accept one another regardless of musical persuasion!

Your personal progress

Every so often, stand back and look at your own progress both as a person and as a leader. Encourage your wife to do the same, and help each other assess areas where effort is required. There may be a particular person in your group to whom you find it hard to relate, and you need to apply yourself to establishing contact and friendship. Perhaps you do not feel comfortable in a teaching capacity, and you need to work at this so that your group can benefit from clear and well-prepared teaching sessions. And what about your marriage? Are you and your wife growing together in leadership? Are you making time for each other? Is communication improving between you? Be honest about your areas of need and set yourself reachable goals knowing that God, who appointed you to leadership, will work with you and in you to bring your desires and actions into harmony with his 'good purpose' (Phil 2:13).

Watch out for potential leadership

Constant assessment of the progress of your group will help you to be on the alert for the emergence of leadership ability. As you listen to people sharing and discussing together you will become aware of those who have a potential teaching gift, or the ability to lead a discussion or gently bring a 'red-herring contributor' back to the subject. You will notice those who have a real care and consideration for others. In this way you will become aware of any in the group who may be potential house-group leaders; it would be good to give them occasional opportunities of taking the house group or 'standing in' for you if you have to be away. Give yourself to those who are potential leaders; spend time with them, build up a relationship with them. Your example as a leader will encourage and enthuse them. Let your minister or elders know if there is someone in your group who is evidently coming forth as a leader; they can pray about him and keep an eye on his progress. When the time comes, he can be approached regarding leadership training. If God has been speaking to him, and you have been encouraging him, he will be willing and ready.

Don't expect too much too soon

A person's ability to make progress depends very much upon his background. Someone who has grown up in a secure home and who has known love and acceptance will be able to respond to God and to your leadership more quickly than someone who has come to faith in Christ from a deeply insecure and loveless background. Such a person may not only have a very low self-image, but may also lack the confidence and trust in God and in other people to take steps forward in relationships or faith. Much groundwork needs to be done in someone like this to build a foundation of truth and love into his life. He has been 'born again', but he may need quite a time in the 'special care unit' before he becomes comfortable in the nursery. Progress may be slow, but with your loving leadership and the care and commitment of the others in the house group it will eventually begin to take place. For someone like this, each small step will be a 'giant leap'. The first time a shy, introverted person invites someone else for a meal—that's progress! The first time a person who has been constantly needing help expresses a desire to help someone else—that's progress!

Remember that the ultimate goal is to bring people to maturity. It will not happen by next Thursday—but it will happen.

PART TWO

For Ministers, Elders and Church Leaders

12

Why house groups?

Over the years at various times in the church's history small groups have been used as a means of discipling God's people, from Martin Luther's 'ecclesiola in ecclesia' ('the little church within the church') at the time of the Reformation to John Wesley's 'class meetings' and the Welsh 'experience meetings' during the nineteenth century. Now, in the twentieth century, we are seeing a tremendous increase in the number of churches using house groups, particularly in South America and South Korea. In England, too, the rising tide of spiritual life amongst the people of God is demanding a greater reality of church life and commitment to one another. In these exciting days when God is restoring his church, men in pastoral leadership need to take seriously the command of the Lord Jesus to 'make disciples'. House groups are God's strategy for this time!

Why house groups?

In England twenty years ago this question would probably have been met with a blank, uncomprehending stare. Not so today! Many churches all over the world have started 'house groups' or 'home groups' or 'cell groups'. Sadly, some churches have jumped onto the 'house-group bandwagon' without a real understanding on the part of leaders and members of what they are meant to be doing, and so they fail to function effectively.

It is vital to build on right foundations. The Lord Jesus gave clear instructions to the apostles about what they were to do. In Matthew 28:19–20 he tells them to 'make disciples of all nations, baptising them in the name of the Father and of the Son and of the Holy Spirit, and teaching them to obey everything I have commanded you'. This 'making of disciples' is the vital task of spiritual leadership. In the New Testament Christians are referred to as 'disciples' over 250 times, and only twice as 'believers'. A disciple means a 'taught' or 'trained' one. This discipling cannot be done 'en masse'. We cannot do better than follow the example of the Lord Jesus, who took a dozen men and gave himself to them—teaching, training, correcting and equipping them.

Closely allied to this 'discipling' is the care of God's people. Peter was specifically told by Jesus to 'feed and take care of [*poimaine*, to shepherd] my sheep (Jn 21:15–17). In Acts 20:28 Paul exhorts the elders at Ephesus to 'keep watch over yourselves and all the flock of which the Holy Spirit has made you overseers. Be shepherds of the church of God, which he bought with his own blood.' This discipling, caring and shepherding of the people of God is an eldership function, but one which also draws in others.

Biblical basis for shared leadership

You will not find a specific verse of scripture which mentions a 'house group', but it is evident from both the Old and New Testaments that God provided a variety of different-sized groups to achieve his purposes in the civil, social and spiritual life of his people.

An example of how God enabled Moses to share out the governmental care of people is seen in Exodus 18:13–27. A careful reading of this passage will show a) the reason why smaller units of care were recommended; b) the basic unit size; c) the qualities necessary in the men who were to be selected as leaders; d) the continuing responsibilities of Moses; e) what he was to teach; and f) what the men's responsibilities were. We should note too that Moses, even with the addition of helpers, did not abdicate his responsibilities, nor did the men carry the full burden and weight on their own; what they could not handle they could refer upwards.

Sharing physical care

Another example of the sharing of responsibility in the physical care of people is seen in Luke 9:12–17. Jesus was able to *teach* a vast crowd which included five thousand men, but when it came to *feeding* them he introduced an arrangement which would ensure that all would be adequately looked after. They were to sit down in groups of about fifty, and only when this was done did Jesus break the bread and fish and give it to the disciples to give some to each group of fifty.

Sharing spiritual care

The same was true of the spiritual care in the New Testament. The early church met both in the temple courts (which would have been large gatherings) and also in their homes. The homes of God's people were widely used in New Testament times; a variety of activities took place in them. A look at the following verses will show this very clearly: Acts 2:46, Acts 12:12, Acts 16:40, Romans 16:4–5, Romans 16:23, 1 Corinthians 16:19, Colossians 4:15 and Philemon 2. Believers freely opened their homes for fellowship and teaching in smaller groups than the gathered church. Here they could enjoy fellowship together, learn and laugh together, pray and worship together. They could be taught the foundation of their faith, and they could ask questions and receive answers. They were committed to one another as God's family, sharing all that they had and being 'one in heart and mind' (Acts 4:32).

A structure of teaching

A 'structure of teaching' was clearly established. This was needed to ensure both the continuity of sound doctrine and a degree of individual care which meant that all God's people would be adequately taught and the truth established in their lives. 2 Timothy 2:2 gives the biblical pattern for the discipling of Christians. *Paul* taught *Timothy* who was to entrust teaching to *reliable men* who were thus qualified to teach *others*. This pattern is very different from the concept that has been traditional in many churches, where the pastor has total responsibility for the teaching, growth and care of the church.

Inadequacy of a 'one-man ministry'

One man in sole charge of a church is an unbiblical situation unless the church is composed of a very small number of people! Even if this were not the case there are two very good reasons why a 'one-man' ministry is inadequate for the shepherding of God's people. Firstly, it is physically, mentally and emotionally impossible for one man to perform all the necessary pastoral tasks in a church. If he has to study, preach, teach, counsel, marry, bury, conduct deacons' meetings, plan programmes, guide the young people, show an interest in the women's meeting, run the men's meeting, sort out the Sunday school, visit the sick, calm the offended and keep everybody happy (including his wife and family), he will very soon find that he is exhausted. His own spiritual life will suffer; time for waiting upon God, building and enjoying the precious relationship with him which is so vital for those who must feed others, will inevitably be lessened by the pressure of many other responsibilities. His family life will suffer because of the very limited time he can spend with his wife and children. He himself will be under pressure continually, and thus unable to give of his best in any of the numerous capacities in which he must function.

The second reason for the inadequacy of a 'one-man' ministry is one which has a far-reaching effect upon the church fellowship which he leads. It is this: *a man who has to spend precious time in organization and in picking up the weak will have no time to build up the strong.* A shared ministry, where a good team of committed house-group leaders are responsible for the 'front-line' pastoral care, will free the pastor (and any other elders) to give himself to building up a strong church, while still being available to deal with matters which are too much for the house-group leaders to handle. He will thus have time to give real input into the lives of the house-group leaders, building them up, teaching them and training more so that the church is ready for growth. Not only will this strengthen the church, but it will help men of ability (who would otherwise sit in the pews while the pastor coped with everything) to realize their full potential. He will also have time to wait on God for the church, to hear God's instruction for the life of his people and receive from God's word and God's heart the vision for what God wants to do with his people in that place.

Your personal reservations

If you are in pastoral leadership of a church and are prayerfully considering the introduction of a house-group system, there may be some personal reservations in your heart in spite of your realization that your church will benefit greatly from such a move. Perhaps you are wondering if the people will think you are opting out of your responsibilities? After all, *you* are paid to pastor the church! Perhaps you are aware that in handing over your flock to be shepherded by house-group leaders you are taking the risk of those leaders proving as adequate as you are, or even (whisper it quietly) *better* than you are—and how will you handle that? These reservations need to be honestly faced, and they relate very much to the matter of your own security in God (see chapter 2). You can be sure that when you take a step in the will of God which is beneficial to his people he will not let you lose by it. God will certainly deal with any wrong attitudes you have in terms of status and reputation. You may realize that your commitment to the growth and good of the church rather than to your own position as pastor may not be as clear-cut as you thought it was when viewed in the light of Philippians 2:5–8. To hand over the immediate pastoral care of your flock to a group of raw house-group leaders is a risk. But it is no greater risk than Jesus took when he entrusted the care of the church to his first apostles in the power of the Holy Spirit—and no greater risk than when he put part of his church into *your* care. It is his church, and any changes which are implemented, when they are carried out at the instigation and in the power of the Holy Spirit, will only be for good.

Change is sometimes painful, especially for the one who is delegating leadership; the fear of feeling 'redundant', the concern of wondering if the new leaders will 'make it' and whether the people will be cared for adequately, all contribute to the reservations you may have in your heart. Bring them into the open. Talk with a brother pastor whose church is functioning well in house groups; visit him and see how it works. Above all, trust the Spirit of God as he leads you and confirms to your heart the rightness of this step in the life of the church.

How house groups will benefit your church

A tree is a good illustration of how house groups function within the church. The trunk of the tree is the congregational gathering for worship and teaching; here is visibility, identity and strength. The branches are the house groups reaching out into the locality, each one a centre for fellowship and sharing. Finally, the twigs are the individual members—and it is the twigs that bear the fruit. All the parts of the tree are essential; the branches support the twigs and feed nourishment through from the trunk and the roots. The house groups are the vital link between the gathered church and its structure of leadership and teaching. The benefits of such a system are many and varied.

Bringing people to maturity

House groups provide an environment which enables each member to grow to maturity in his Christian life. The caring, sharing and loving he experiences, the opportunity for participation in a non-critical atmosphere and the encouragement of his leader all combine to promote spiritual and emotional growth.

Training people for spiritual warfare

The Christian life is a battle. All too often Christians, finding themselves under attack from Satan in various areas of their lives, struggle on alone or make an appointment with the pastor. The pastor may be able to help them, but he is a busy man and not always available to give them subsequent ongoing support. A Christian who is part of a caring house group, under the leadership of a man who is personally involved with him on a regular basis, is in a far stronger position. Together the house group can pray against the activity of the enemy in the life of any one of its members. The house-group leader can regularly remind the person under attack of the biblical principles which are the foundation of his faith, of the victory of Jesus over Satan, of the strength and power available through the Holy Spirit— and of the fact that he is not alone, but part of a group which can stand together against the enemy on his behalf.

In evangelism, too, the group can join together to wage intercessory warfare for those who are hearing the gospel through its members or through others in the church. If there is to be a special outreach service each house group can pray as a fighting unit; this kind of intercession takes ground from the enemy and opens the way for unbelievers to respond to the gospel.

Producing genuine relationships

We are all 'members of one body' (Eph 4:25) and the house-group 'family' is the place where qualities such as forbearance, forgiveness, patience, gentleness and love are worked out. Jesus prayed that his people would be one, and said that this would be a demonstration to the world that God had sent him (Jn 17:23). This kind of unity can only come about when people learn to accept one another with all their individual peculiarities and differences; the house group provides a place where close, genuine relationships can blossom and grow.

Meeting practical needs in the church

A church with house groups has a ready-made system of teams to tackle anything. In our own church, one house group is responsible each week for cleaning the church halls. As we have eighteen house groups, the job only has to be done once every few months by each house group. When we have a wedding in the church, each house group provides a part of the wedding meal. A list is given to each house-group leader and his wife by our 'catering co-ordinator'. They are then responsible for allocating the work to the members of their group. For instance, five people will provide a savoury flan each, five people will supply a bowl of salad each and five more will provide a trifle or a gateau each. The rest will provide crisps, nuts, rolls or whatever else is needed. When the contributions from all the house groups are assembled on the day of the wedding the resulting feast is magnificent! This kind of practical service is extra to the mutual caring and sharing which is taking place all the time between house-group members.

The importance of preparation

Introducing house groups into your church is a step which requires much groundwork and preparation. You as pastor or elder, together with any other elders or deacons in leadership, need to be fully convinced in your own mind that this is the will of God for your church. You will need to pray and wait on God for this. You will find it helpful, as we said earlier, to visit churches where house groups are working well and to visit one or two of their groups.

You will need to spend time teaching and preparing the church, and answering innumerable questions! At the same time you will need to be training house-group leaders. A date will need to be set for the commencement of the groups, and decisions made about geography and numbers. We will look at these preparations in more detail in the next two chapters.

13

Teaching the church about house groups

When you as pastor, together with the rest of your church leadership, have prayed and waited on God regarding the matter of house groups, and have become convinced that this is the way forward for your church, what steps should you take? We have outlined the practical steps, with particular attention to the selection and training of house-group leaders, in the next chapter. But one of the most important things is to share with the whole church exactly what you are planning to do and why, and it is this aspect which we shall consider now.

Communicate positively

It is essential for the people (not just the leaders you are training) to have a clear understanding of the reason for the introduction of house groups into the church. This needs to be communicated in a positive and clear way. It may be helpful to use some of the material in chapters 1, 4, 12 and 14 of this book, together with material from this chapter, as a teaching basis covering several weeks.

What you will need to teach about house groups

You will need to share with people the biblical basis for shared leadership and the need for this in increasing measure as the church grows; to teach them that a house group is not 'just another meeting' but a group of people in committed relationship functioning as part of the total life of the church (the 'tree' illustration from chapter 12 may be helpful here); that the purpose of a house group is to bring its members to maturity in every level of their lives; about the kind of activities which will take place in the groups; and that the house group is not for the casual church attender but for those who are born again and committed members of the church. You will need to teach that the members of the house group are to be committed to one another and to regular attendance and participation in the life of the group.

A change in the weekly programme

You will need to make it clear that the introduction of house groups is not one more thing to be added on to the existing programme. Experience has shown that it is best if the groups meet at least weekly. Most churches have found that with the introduction of house groups the midweek prayer meeting or Bible study is no longer necessary— though it will be right at times to call the church together for prayer in addition to the groups. In our own church once a month the Sunday evening service takes the form of a prayer evening. It is then that we pray as a church for our nation, for evangelism in our area and for specific needs in the fellowship. This is reinforced by prayer in the house groups in the intervening weeks. We may not always keep to this programme; we want to be flexible and to follow the Spirit's leading. But at the present moment this way of corporate praying is right for us.

It is also important to make time for social gatherings (sometimes two or three house groups together), which provide opportunities to promote fellowship between people in different house groups. We mentioned in an earlier chapter that sometimes two of our groups will get together, one group preparing and serving a meal for the other group. This will be reciprocated a few weeks later.

The groups usually use the church hall for this kind of get-together—very few front rooms can cope!

A change in the leadership structure

You will need to teach that there must be a genuine recognition of the lordship of Jesus and an obedience to and receiving of the ministry of God's shepherds and leaders. People will need to hear about the importance of being committed to their house-group leader. Some will find this hard, particularly those who have been used to 'calling the pastor' for every need and emergency. One dear elderly lady in our own fellowship had great difficulty accepting that her house-group leader was the one who was now caring for her on a regular basis. She felt that her pastor had abandoned her! It took three years of loving care from her house-group leader and the other members of her group to convince her that, far from being abandoned, she was now being cared for more adequately than before. Older church members who have been consistently 'pastor-orientated' may need to be taught this gently but persistently for a long time!

People will need teaching, as we said earlier, that house groups are now the way the church will be pastored. No longer is there a 'loose' membership with house groups as an optional extra. The groups are for committed people, with the elders as the 'gateway' through which people are put into groups. For some people who have remained on the fringe of the church for many years this may be a time of decision. There is a possibility that some may leave. Some will recognize for the first time their need for real commitment to the Lord and to his people. Some, realizing the true nature of the church, may acknowledge for the first time their need of salvation and forgiveness.

Objections may be raised

Your congregation will want to ask questions, and opportunity needs to be given for this. They will expect you to have answers! Many of their questions will in fact be answered as you teach from the material in this book. Some people may raise objections to the whole concept of house groups, and we will now look at some of those.

'Surely it will divide the church into cliques?'

Those who are afraid of this need to be shown that house groups will, in fact, foster strong relationships rather than clique-ish groups; and that strong and committed relationships are a good thing. The kind of 'cliques' usually meant when this objection is raised are those little groups which either leave others feeling 'out in the cold' or become hot-beds of gossip and criticism. Proper teaching and commitment should ensure that neither of these things happen as a result of the introduction of house groups. In fact, people who learn to make good relationships in a smaller group usually relate better to people generally—which makes 'cliques' even less likely to form.

'What about the prayer meeting?'

Some people genuinely feel that if house groups are taking the place of the weekly prayer meeting it means that the church is taking a backward step and that corporate prayer will be neglected. They need to know that this is not the case; that there will be effective prayer taking place in the house groups and that the church will still come together for prayer at specific times—perhaps on a Sunday at regular intervals, which we mentioned earlier as being the practice in our own fellowship.

'Why should the elders decide which groups we go into—that's not democratic!'

No, it's *not* democratic—but democracy is not a biblical

concept. Hebrews 13:17 states that those in leadership must give account of their flock. God puts elders over the church to rule with love, and gives them wisdom to do so. Obedience to them is part of each church member's commitment. The elders will, after prayer, designate people to the groups which they feel will benefit them most; their counsel needs to be received.

'We've heard dreadful stories about shepherding and authority!'

So have we all; and there is no doubt that in some situations authority has been badly mishandled. We have all heard about people who couldn't change their wallpaper, move their furniture or go on holiday without asking their elders or leaders! It is also a fact that Satan delights in proliferating these tales in order to make God's people wary of authority in any form; remember that Satan rebelled against authority from the very beginning—and that has not changed. He will seek to make loving and wise leadership appear tyrannical and harsh. An illustration may help here. 'The elders at that church stopped my neighbour's daughter going out with her boyfriend—and he's *such* a nice fellow. I think it's disgusting to interfere in people's lives like that!' What this person did not know is that the said boyfriend is not a Christian and the neighbour's daughter *is*. She had become involved with him and the elders of her church had warned her that this relationship was wrong in the sight of God and a danger to her spiritual life. She had recognized the truth of this, repented and finished with her boyfriend. Hence the distorted tale, which was soon going round the neighbourhood!

Some of the stories do sound dreadful until investigated. For instance, 'We knew a family who had to tell the elders exactly what they were earning—and the elders said they weren't to spend any money without asking permission!' The facts in this case were that the couple in question, both born-again believers, were constantly in debt, unable to control their spending and quite unable to manage their finances. When they became committed members of a church which was moving in the Spirit, the love and care which they experienced prompted them to share their difficulties (which had already become evident) with the elders, who appointed one of their number—a man with financial skills—to look into the couple's problems. He helped them to draw up a realistic budget plan, and they were required to keep to this ('they can't spend any money without asking permission!') in order to achieve a stable financial position. The church also made them a monetary gift which cleared a large part of their debts. It was necessary to make them accountable to the elder who was helping them until they had learned how to manage their money. They were willing and glad for this, though finding it hard at times during the process. Firm authority—yes! Hard, tyrannical and unloving—no! But to those who only heard a smattering of the truth, a dreadful example of 'heavy shepherding'.

We need to recognize that many of the 'tales' which we hear are half-truths embellished by Christians who should know better than to repeat gossip. If you, as pastor or elder, hear a story which worries you, go to the people themselves and ask what the truth is. If it is to do with folk from another church, go to the elders of that church and find out what is *really* happening. Elders who are walking in the light before God and one another will be glad to answer your questions.

At some times and in some places there has indeed been a wrong use of authority and people have suffered as a consequence. But do not let that obscure the fact that scriptural authority is a *security*, not a threat, for the people of God. House-group leaders have an authority which is delegated to them by their pastor and/or elders, and they will be accountable to them for the people in their groups. Encourage your church members to see this as loving and caring authority which will build them up and bring them security.

Gossip is destructive

We have seen in the previous section the harm which can be caused by repeating gossip. Teach your people that criticism and gossip is destructive and harmful. Criticism of their new house-group leaders (who may well make mistakes) or of the elders who have brought in this new system (which may well take time to get off the ground successfully) will be unhelpful both to those who indulge in it and to those against whom it is directed. Share with them the fact that real commitment means that they will pray, not criticize; love, not condemn.

14

Planning and starting house groups in your church

In this chapter we will look at the practical steps which will need to be taken if you are planning to start house groups in your church. In the previous chapter we dealt with the matter of teaching the church about the biblical basis for shared leadership, the function and aims of the house groups and the effect they will have on the life of the church. While you are doing this (and answering the innumerable questions which will be asked) there will be other practical decisions to make. We shall be looking at those in this chapter. When the plans are finalized you will want to share them with the church so that everyone knows how the new set-up will work and be aware of their place in it.

The importance of leadership

God's provision for the care of his people in the local church is Holy Spirit-anointed eldership. The house-group leader will be appointed and supported by the pastor and elders, and will be responsible to them for the basic pastoral needs of his group. Unless it is impossible for geographical or other reasons, it is best if the group meets in the leader's home. This will help to underline the importance of this relationship and the need to recognize and receive his spiritual authority. The group will also have the opportunity of seeing how he and his wife and family live; this teaching by example is a vital part of church life.

Selection and training of house-group leaders

It is advisable to begin selecting and training leaders before preparing the church for the introduction of house groups. Right leadership in the work of God is crucial and the success of the groups will be largely dependent on the quality of the leadership appointed. When forming a group of 'trainees' it is best to make clear that attending the training sessions does not automatically or immediately qualify a person for leadership. It is better to delay than to appoint the wrong people.

Who should lead house groups?

House-group discipling and care is 'home' centred, and is particularly designed to bring people together in all-age 'family' units—young, middle-aged, elderly, single and married; and, as we said earlier, it is best if house-group leaders are married couples able to use their own homes. It is possible for a member's home to be used if distance or lack of suitable space makes the leader's own home unsuitable. A single man could also function in leadership. The elders could assign a married couple or a godly woman to assist where needed; but this situation, as in the situation of a member's home being used rather than the leader's, should be thought of as an exception rather than the rule.

In our own church we would not appoint a single woman as house-group leader; we do not feel that a woman is emotionally equipped to carry alone the task and responsibility of this kind of leadership. We gladly recognize the tremendous ability of women in many fields, and their invaluable contribution to house-group life, and would be happy about a woman occasionally taking a house-group evening. But it seems clear from the New Testament that the leadership care of the people of God is the task of men.

What are the necessary qualities for a house-group leader?

It is not one factor but many which go towards making a person suitable to lead others. The greater the responsibility the more one would look to see these abilities and qualities of character in a person. In this section we shall look at those abilities and qualities which are vital to leadership. A man and his wife would not be disqualified if all these are not present in abundant measure, but if there is no evidence of them one would need to think again. We are not advising you to look for some kind of spiritual 'Superman' but rather seeking to give you an overall impression of the kind of person who can be trained and taught to lead others. A word of caution may be needed for those churches who have had house groups for some time and are wanting now to train more new leaders. It is only natural that when you think of new house-group leaders you will be comparing them with existing leaders. Remember that those leaders have probably had several years' experience and the benefit of considerable input from the elders; you will need to bear this in mind and not set your standards by what the leaders are like *now* but by what they were like two or three years ago!

Some essential requirements for leadership

It is essential that someone who is being considered for leadership has left the spiritual nursery school! Hebrews 5:11–6:3 makes it clear that Paul expected people to have moved on to teaching others after a certain length of time, and he was saddened to see that they still needed to be taught the elementary truths all over again. Without expounding this passage in full, it is evident that a person who is not living in the reality of these truths has not even progressed beyond the 'elementary' or 'ABC' stage. It is here that we must begin. You should consider the following points when you are considering people for leadership:

a) Do they show a heart of repentance toward God—that is, not only the repentance that precedes salvation, but a turning from all that is sinful on an ongoing basis?
b) Do they have a genuine faith in God—for salvation *and* for daily life; are they people of faith?
c) Have they been baptized by immersion as believers and are they showing the fruit of it in daily life?
d) Have they been baptized in the Holy Spirit and are they 'open to God' in worship, spiritual gifts, and so on?
e) Is their life characterized by 'resurrection'— that is, a real confidence in the risen Lord Jesus?
f) Have they a reverence for God, his statutes and his word; an ability to distinguish good from evil; an awareness that they are accountable to God?

These are all basics for a Christian, before he is even considered for leadership!

As well as fulfilling these basic requirements, it is important that a potential leader should have an ability to lead and teach others. Not everyone has the ability to lead; it is one of the gifts which God gives (see Romans 12:6–8). The word 'leadership' in verse 8 carries the meaning 'he who is placed in front'. Qualities which are essential for those who are 'placed in front' of others have to do with character as well as ability.

Several passages of Scripture bear this out. In Exodus 18:21 we see that Moses was to look for three things in the men he appointed to leadership. They were to be capable, God-fearing and trustworthy. The first word has to do with the ability to manage things well. The Hebrew word translated 'capable' (*chayil*) is used in Genesis 47:6. Pharaoh wisely wanted someone of 'special ability' to look after his own livestock. A man who cannot properly manage his own family, work or home, is not going to manage a house group either! The second word has to do with a man's view of God. You can safely commit people into the hands of someone who fears God. The third word indicates the kind of person who is 'straight'—he won't say one thing to your face and another thing behind your back. Neither will he seek favour from some and be unnecessarily harsh with others. A good shepherd loves all the sheep to the same degree.

In 2 Timothy 2:2 Paul points out two requirements for leaders: '*reliable* men who will also be *qualified to teach others*'. The word translated as 'reliable' describes someone who can be trusted. You can depend on him; he is loyal. He will keep his word. The second word (Greek: *hikanos*) has to do with a person's competence. Paul is very definite that truth needs to be taught—it is a sacred deposit to be handed down and entrusted to every new generation of believers. A house-group leader does not need to be a pastor/teacher to a congregation, but he does need to be competent (or have the ability to become so) in teaching a handful of people. That means he must have a love for the word of God, an ability to understand it and the teaching which is brought by the eldership, and an aptitude for helping people to understand and enter into truth. Bezalel and Oholiab are examples of this (see Exodus 35:35). This verse also shows how truth is to be received; not through a correspondence course or private study, but in the interaction of leaders together.

Let's look briefly at three more passages. Ephesians 4:11–12 sets out the combined task of apostles, prophets, evangelists, pastors and teachers. Although these verses do not specifically refer to house-group leaders, there is a vital principle here; these ministries are to 'prepare God's people for works of service' (v.12). There is a clear goal in view! Leaders do not exist for themselves but to prepare people. That means they must have an ability to relate openly and lovingly with other people; to be real examples that others can follow.

Now look at 1 Timothy 3:1–7. This has to do with elders—but again the principles hold good for all who would serve God's people. Verses 4 and 5 indicate the importance of a man's own home and family being right. Our homes are 'mini training-schools' for the bigger thing.

Is there clear evidence in those you plan to bring into leadership that they are working at this area of their lives?

Finally, look at Mark 10:42–45 and see the difference between those who rule in God's kingdom and those who rule in the worldly system. There is no place in God's kingdom for competitiveness, envy, jealousy and striving to be 'someone'. Jesus tells us that coming into leadership means *serving*; serving those in eldership and serving those in your house group. There are three main words for a 'servant' in the New Testament: *doulos*—meaning a slave, speaking of a submissive heart; *diakonos*—meaning to render service; and *latreuo*—which has to do with sacrifice and worship. True service can only flow from a servant heart, and when it does it will bless others and also be a ministry of worship to the Lord.

To sum up: leaders are men and women with shepherd hearts who will care for, restore, guide, protect and provide for God's people. A useful exercise which will help you to detect the presence or absence of some of these qualities in your trainee leaders is to ask them to look at Exodus 18:17–27. Verse 20 speaks of a) teaching the people the decrees and laws, b) showing them the way to live, and c) showing them the duties they are to perform. Ask your trainee leaders to do this in their 'imaginary' house group; what kinds of things would they put under these three headings? It would also be helpful for them to study Psalm 23 and note down everything they can about how the shepherd cares for his people.

Wives are important

What has been written above has related specifically to the house-group leader. But what about his wife? Her role is basically supportive, and is described in more detail in chapter 3. Her main responsibility is to share her husband's vision and be a real support and encouragement to him. If she is not hospitable, caring and one with him in her desire to see God's people grow, then however good the man is, sadly such a couple would not be ready or suitable to come into leadership.

The initial approach

We spoke earlier of the advisability of initiating leadership training as early as possible, certainly before you begin to introduce the concept of house groups to the church. This will mean taking the prospective leaders into your confidence and sharing your vision with them. When you approach them with regard to possible leadership you may find that some who are eminently suited for leadership may be utterly taken aback at the thought! They will need to be encouraged and assured of your confidence in them and that they will not be left to cope alone. They would find it of real value to read through Part 1 of this book to get some idea of what is involved. The whole purpose of the training and the ongoing relationship with the elders is to provide support and encouragement.

A check list

To summarize, use the following check list of qualities when considering a prospective house-group leader:

Caring   Baptized in water
Competent to teach   Baptized in the Holy Spirit
Able to relate to people   Open to God
Hospitable   Free in worship and gifts
Reliable   A serving heart
Loyal   Right home and family life
Hates sin   Submissive spirit
Loves God   Teachable

You can only shepherd committed sheep

Who should go into the house groups? As we have seen throughout this book, it is only possible to shepherd and care for people where there is a right basis. The groups are essentially intended for the care of God's people who are committed to the spiritual leadership of the church. This means that not everyone who comes into the church for a Sunday service is automatically a member of the church or eligible to go into a house group. Membership of a group should be on the basis of a clear experience of salvation and a real commitment to the body of Christ and the leadership. It is from this number that you will need to form your house groups. If there is uncertainty as to who comes into this category, it may be valuable and helpful to take everyone through some basic teaching on what it means to be part of the church. The manual, *How to Join the Church*, published by Coastlands Trust, or Arthur Wallis' book, *Living God's Way*, would be a suitable basis for this type of teaching. Once the house groups are established new Christians and new members joining the church should be taken through such a teaching book either individually or as a commitment group during their first few weeks as members. (This can run concurrently with their membership of a house group; we feel that people need to be placed in a house group as early as possible in order to feel part of the church. This applies particularly to new Christians, who need real support, fellowship and love in their early days.)

Who goes where?

There is no 'formula' for deciding who should go into which house group. As elders, *you* must make the decision as to where people are to be placed. There are four specific factors which you will need to take into consideration:
1) The need for balanced groups in terms of a) age, b) marrieds and singles, c) spiritually mature and new Christians.
2) The need for people who live near each other to be in the same group. This will facilitate transport and also make day-to-day care and relationship between the group members much easier.

3) The need to recognize that some people will be helped by and respond to one leader more than another.

4) The need for each group to have a musician or someone competent to lead singing.

You will also need to consider three other points: the minimum age for which you are going to cater; whether young people from church families should go into the same group as their parents; and baby-sitting provision for married couples with small children.

Firstly, the age factor. There is a great deal to be said for not letting the age for house-group attendance drop below fourteen years. Few young people are ready below that age for the kind of sharing which will take place in house groups. Secondly, the matter of parents and children. Experience has shown that parents and their teenage children are able to share with much greater ease when they are not in the same group. It's important for young people to grow up—not necessarily independently of their parents, but certainly not in precisely the same soil! Finally, couples with small children. If the house groups meet on two different nights, it should not be too difficult (as we have explained earlier in chapter 6) to arrange a baby-sitting rota so that couples with small children can go together to the same group. In our own church the baby-sitting rota is in the care of one of our house-group leaders and his wife. When new people come into a house group they are put in touch with Laurie and Maggie who will then go through the list of baby-sitting volunteers to find someone who is free on the appropriate night. Some people are able to baby-sit every week; some are available for two Thursdays each month, which means that someone else would need to be found for the other two Thursdays. The baby-sitting rota is a masterpiece of organization, and needs to be handled efficiently! The matter of transport may also need attention, and lifts may need to be arranged for those who are elderly or who are not able to reach their house-group meeting easily for one reason or another.

Setting a date

It is a good idea to settle on a specific time a few months ahead for the actual commencement of house groups, so that the teaching and orientation of the church and the training of the house-group leaders can work towards a given date. In our own church we decided to commence house groups in early September, when everyone had returned from their summer holidays. This made a good starting point, coinciding with the beginning of the school year.

Forming the groups

Having made decisions about the matters just mentioned, you will need to make the allocations. The wisest thing would probably be for the elders to prayerfully draw up a provisional list, taking into account the factors of balance, geography, individuality and music (referred to above). The list could then be shared with those trainee house-group leaders you feel are ready for leadership. If they have any particular insights or observations which are seen to be helpful and relevant the list can be amended as necessary.

Finally, bring it to the church and state that this is where people will be allocated. Unless there are very good reasons why someone should be moved (and there may be some factor of which you are not aware, for example, a student having evening classes on the particular night that the group to which he has been allocated meets), it would be wise *not* to give people the option of saying, 'I would rather be in Derek's and not Andrew's group'. If it does happen that after several months a person obviously doesn't 'fit' a group, then you could make adjustment. There is no need to blame anybody if this becomes necessary.

Coping with growth

Living things grow! The church should be growing both in spiritual maturity and in numbers. As elders you will need to prepare for this. Be on the look-out for emerging leaders. Encourage your house-group leaders to give likely men in their groups the opportunity to share, lead the worship or give teaching. Potential leaders will become apparent. It is a good thing to start training leaders as soon as it becomes evident that you will be needing new house group in three or four months' time.

You will need to decide on a policy regarding growth. There are two options. You can let one house group grow and grow by adding new members to it—and then divide it into two groups. Or you can add to them all over a period of time and then form a new group by taking a few people from all or most of the groups. Both methods have points to commend them. In the former case those in the new group will already have a relationship with each other and this can be an advantage; but if the growing stage from, say, fifteen to thirty takes several months it can put a strain on the leader and his wife—and on the seating capacity of the front room! In the end you will have to decide which plan suits your situation best; or you may want to adopt both at different times according to your needs as a church.

The opening night

When the evening actually arrives for house groups to commence there will be nothing for you to do. But don't sit at home biting your nails! Pray for the activities going on in the various front rooms of those who are launching out into leadership for the first time. Read chapter 4 of this book to give you a clearer idea of what may actually be happening. Be on hand to particularly encourage your new leaders during the early weeks. They will be experiencing for the first time the joys and sorrows which are an inevitable part of life for those involved in the pastoral care of people. When we began house groups, one of our new leaders came with his wife to see us, and they said with wry grins, 'Now we know what it's been like for *you* for the past nine years!'

15

Your care of the house-group leader

The security of a church is greatly dependent upon the
unity and mutual care of its leadership. When you appoint
house-group leaders to help you with the care of the church
they will need to know that you are right behind them,
supporting them in every way possible. For some it will be
their first experience of leadership responsibility; they will
need to know that you are available to a house-group
leader needing help, but at the same time they must learn to
lead. If a leader comes running to you with every little crisis
('Jane and Sally aren't speaking to each other—it's making
house group nights very difficult!'), he will not grow in his
ability to lead and to handle people. He must learn to help
Jane and Sally resolve their problem in a biblical manner!
But if there is a major crisis he will need to know that you
are ready to come into the situation with him. The members
of the house group will feel secure in knowing that there is
constant and frequent liaison between their house-group
leader and the pastor and elders of the church. Jesus required the men whom he sent out to return to him frequently
to report their progress and receive his encouragement and
help (Mt 17:19, Lk 10:17) and later the apostles kept in
constant touch with those who were ministering to the
churches (Acts 8:14, 1 Thess 3:6). In the same way you
must maintain constant contact with those who are leading
under you. It is evident from the epistles of Paul to both
Timothy and Titus that Paul often had to advise his leaders
by letter, due to distance, communication problems and

the unique, far-flung situation of the early church. *You* should not have to resort to this! Your diary needs to be programmed with the needs of your house-group leaders as a priority.

Regular meetings

In the initial stages of establishing house groups there is a great deal in favour of elders meeting with house-group leaders on a weekly basis—preferably in the earlier part of the week and before the house-group meeting. It is a good idea to have a quarterly programme prepared in advance with evenings planned for leaders alone and at other times with their wives. In large churches with a number of house groups and several elders there is value in meeting at times in smaller groups, one elder with two or three house-group leaders. From time to time all the leaders with their wives may be brought together for a specially planned teaching evening to receive ministry on subjects which are suited to the needs at that time. This may sound quite demanding and you may wonder how to fit it in with other eldership commitments, particularly if not all the elders are full-time. However, long-term planning with good communication should help. A quarterly programme could be planned and circulated as follows:

QUARTERLY PROGRAMME : JANUARY–MARCH

Tues Jan 1	Elders and house-group leaders
Tues Jan 8	Elders and house-group leaders in small groups
Tues Jan 15	Elders and house-group leaders
Tues Jan 22	Elders and house-group leaders with their wives in small groups for a meal together
Tues Jan 29	Elders and house-group leaders
Tues Feb 5	Administration evening

Tues Feb 12	Elders and house-group leaders
Tues Feb 19	Elders and house-group leaders in small groups
Tues Feb 26	Elders and house-group leaders and their wives
Tues Mar 5	Elders and house-group leaders
Tues Mar 12	Elders and house-group leaders in small groups
Tues Mar 26	Teaching evening for all in leadership and their wives (Subject: How to help people with their devotional life)

You will notice that a church administration evening has been fitted in; this would probably not include house-group leaders, but it would take the pressure off the elders to find another evening for this. If the elders are not able to meet during the day time, the programme would need to be modified so that they could meet on their own twice a month. The programme outlined above is only a suggestion and you will be able to adapt it to suit your own situation. But it serves to illustrate the point that forethought and planning are vitally necessary. You may need to change the programme as the house groups develop. As the leaders become more established and experienced it may be necessary to meet only every other week. This frees one of the evenings for them to visit individual members of their groups or to prepare for the house-group meeting; we have found this works well in our own fellowship.

When you meet together

When elders and house-group leaders meet together, what should you do? These meetings should be times for sharing needs and any problems in the group, followed by prayer for them. The elders should give direction about any special teaching or matters to be shared for the coming week. There is great value in just being together, worshipping, sharing (especially from the elders) things that God is saying, waiting on God together, enjoying one another's company and developing friendship and relationship together.

Individual care

In addition to a regular evening together there will need to be times when an elder and his wife spend time with the house-group leader and his wife just as two couples. The ideal situation is to have a meal together and then over coffee chat about how they are getting on, the difficulties and encouragements they are experiencing and how individuals in the group are progressing. The importance of the elders' relationship with the house-group leaders cannot be over-stated—it is the key to the ongoing care of the church. The elders need to help each house-group leader develop his strengths and conquer his weaknesses, and for this mutual confidence and honest communication is very important. Talk it through with him if he feels that he has 'blown it' in a situation; help him to learn from it something which will help him on future occasions. Reassure him that you are there to help him and to take the ultimate responsibility for the group; but encourage him continually in his own growth as a leader.

The number of elders and house-group leaders will obviously dictate how frequently you will be able to see each other on a one-to-one basis, but it is important to do so. A notebook with a page for each house group member will help elders to keep their memories fresh about the progress of individuals within the groups.

If, as elders, you sense that a leader and his wife are under pressure (see chapter 2 for possible causes) or are not coping adequately, or that difficulties are being experienced in the group, you must not ignore the warning signs. You will need to handle the situation wisely and find out what is causing the problem. The needs of the house-group leaders must be your first line of duty. Your care of them will determine how they care for their groups.

Assessing progress

When Jesus sent out the twelve with specific instructions he wanted a report on what they had done (Lk 9:10). He wanted to know whether the task he had given them had been done satisfactorily. Elders are to do the same.

Periodically, with the house-group leaders' full knowledge, you will need to arrange to visit the groups on a rota basis; then to talk through what you observe—both good and bad. It is probably not wise to do this for the first few months as both leaders and groups need a chance to settle down.

There is value in having written reports. You may want this to be a weekly report or only to be used occasionally, but it can be a useful means of checking on the progress of the group—especially if you are not able to meet with the leaders as frequently as every week. It is a great help to the house-group leader to know that he can put something down on paper and that it will reach his busy elders! This is a sample of a report sheet which we have used:

HOUSE GROUP LEADER'S REPORT

Name .... Number in group ....
Week commencing Sunday ....
1. HOUSE-GROUP MEETING
a) Main activities. (Be specific, i.e. if a Bible study: who
led it? What did you study? What conclusions did you
come to? Etc.)
b) Did anything significant happen?
c) Who didn't attend?
d) Were you happy about the evening? Was there
anything that disappointed you?
e) Is there any member about whom you need to see
the elders?

2. TUESDAY PASTORAL OR LEADERS' EVENING
a) Pastoral evening. (Give a brief report, i.e. person you visited, any problems or encouragements.)
b) Leaders' evening. (Comments or observations.)

These reports will need to be followed up with the house-group leader. Giving an honest report is not easy; but the elders need to have a clear picture of the group's growth, limitations and general health. Asking 'How is the group, Michael?' and receiving the answer 'Fine' is not satisfactory! It conveys nothing at all. You must encourage and help your house-group leader to share honestly. He may find it difficult to tell you about his failures, disappointments or bad handling of situations or lack of progress with people in case you come down hard on him or feel he is inadequate for the job. We live in a very competitive world and we are all part of it! However, it has to be communicated to Michael that we are not ruled by the world's principles of competitiveness but by the principles of honesty and commitment which operate in the kingdom of God. He must learn to share honestly with you, so that matters can be talked through openly and helpfully as we suggested earlier in the chapter.

Other ways of supporting leaders

Some group leaders will take to leading and teaching like ducks to water, but others will struggle for hours and not feel they have anything very helpful to share with their groups. There are several constructive ways in which you can help them.
1) Going over the Sunday ministry and talking through particular matters which need emphasis; suggesting questions.
2) Suggesting study guides or published notes which are suited to group study. Some of these are mentioned in chapter 5.

3) Duplicating notes yourself, with questions for the group to discuss.
4) Where leaders' training days are arranged in the area there is great value in attending as a group of elders and house-group leaders. In these days when God is restoring his church there are more and more of these training days being arranged by men with clear apostolic ministry, and they will be of invaluable help to new leaders.

You are a vital source of instruction for your house-group leaders. You can teach them to pray with people and minister with expectant faith. You can teach them to bring people into the baptism with the Holy Spirit. If possible, have the house-group leader with you if you are ministering to someone in his group whether it is for counselling, deliverance ministry or some other need. He will learn from you how to help the people in his care.

Share your vision

It is very important for the house-group leaders to know the heart and vision of the elders. Jesus once had to rebuke two of his disciples because of their judging and condemning attitude (Lk 9:55, see footnote NIV). They had not understood what was in his heart, 'to save men's lives, not to destroy them'. It is clear from Ephesians 6:21 and Colossians 4:7–9 that Tychicus was a man whom Paul could trust to share his vision with others. Paul could not go personally to Colossae and Ephesus, but Tychicus communicated to the believers there what Paul had in his heart. Your house-group leaders need to share your vision for the church; through them the vision will reach the believers in their group.

Share your understanding

The house-group leaders will need to know your thinking on a whole range of issues which, whilst they are not foundational, will nevertheless often crop up in house groups. If the leaders are to represent the views of the eldership they will need to discuss matters such as the following:

    Worldliness
    Sunday—its observance
    Head covering
    Drink
    Dispensationalism
    Tithing and offerings
    Divorce
    Family planning
    Predestination
    Doctrine of the second coming

Over a period of time, or even as an adjunct to the training programme, these matters need to be talked about, the Scriptures examined and the views of the eldership understood so that they can be communicated in the house group.

Relationship is vital

Does all this sound too much like an employer/employee type of situation? Putting it down on paper could give that impression; but it is not to be anything like that. The relationship between you and your house-group leaders, as it is committed to God, will develop and grow into a deep and genuine love and friendship.

Where do you go from here?

You have now come to the end of the book; and you have seen how house groups can function to benefit each church member. Is this the way forward for your church? Is this the means God wants to use to enable you to build up a strong and stable fellowship, a 'people of God prepared for works of service'?

Bibliography

Arnold Bell, *How to Be Sure of the Bible* (Coastlands Trust 1984).

Cyril Bridgland, *Pocket Guide to the Old Testament* (Inter-Varsity Press 1982).

James Dobson, *Dare to Discipline* (Kingsway Publications 1971).

James Dobson, *Hide or Seek* (Hodder & Stoughton 1982).

James Dobson, *Preparing for Adolescence* (Kingsway Publications 1982).

Francis Foulkes, *Pocket Guide to the New Testament* (Inter-Varsity Press 1978).

Dale Garratt, *The Pleasure of Your Company* (Kingsway Publications 1983).

Richard Haydon-Knowell, *How to Join the Church* (Coastlands Trust 1981).

Graham Kendrick, *Worship* (Kingsway Publications 1984).

Tim & Beverly LaHaye, *The Act of Marriage* (Marshall, Morgan & Scott 1985).

Tim LaHaye, *How to be Happy Though Married* (Tyndale House 1968).

Looking After Yourself (Health Education Council booklet 1979).

Josh McDowell, *Givers, Takers and Other Kinds of Lovers* (Kingsway Publications 1981).

Bruce Milne, *Know the Truth* (Inter-Varsity Press 1982).

James I. Packer, *Knowing God* (Hodder & Stoughton 1973).

John Powell, *Why Am I Afraid to Tell You Who I Am?* (Fontana 1975).

Phil Rogers, *How to Be a Worshipper* (Coastlands Trust 1984).

Philip Stanton, *How to Study the Bible* (Coastlands Trust 1984).

Charles Swindoll, *Strike the Original Match* (Kingsway Publications 1983).

Peter Thompson, *Triumphing Under Stress* (Kingsway Publications 1981).

Arthur Wallis, *Living God's Way* (Kingsway Publications 1984).

Ann Warren, *Marriage in the Balance* (Kingsway Publications 1981).

Restoration in the Church

by Terry Virgo

God is restoring his church. Many are now seeing the need to apply New Testament principles to their church structures and time-honoured traditions. Flexibility and freedom are on the increase.

This book takes an inside look at what has been called 'the house church movement' and reveals how amazing growth has come from a rediscovery of Scripture's teaching on ministries in the church. Whatever our situation, we will find a fresh challenge in what the author has to say.

- ☐ The traditional evangelical is reminded that restoration is rooted in the orthodox teaching of the Reformers.

- ☐ The charismatic is asked not to stop with personal gifts but to go on to embrace the ministries of apostle and prophet.

- ☐ Those already committed to restoration are urged to be watchful, avoiding complacency and ready to move on to whatever God has in store.

Terry Virgo is based at Clarendon Church, Hove, Brighton. A frequent visitor to many countries with the message of restoration, he is highly respected for his ministry to church leaders in various denominations, and is a popular speaker at Bible Weeks each year. He is married with five children.

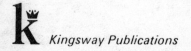

Kingsway Publications